in Memory of
Eleanor Gordon

The art of jewelry design

Production Jewelry by 20 top designers

Q

Quarry books, a division of Rockport Publishers
Distributed by North Light Books, Cincinnati, Ohio
EVANSTON, ILLINOIS 60201

First published in the United States of America by:
Quarry Books, an imprint of
Rockport Publishers, Inc.
146 Granite Street
Rockport, Massachusetts 01966-1299
Telephone: (508) 546-9590
Fax: (508) 546-7141

Distributed to the book trade and art trade in the United States by:
North Light, an imprint of
F & W Publications
1507 Dana Avenue
Cincinnati, Ohio 45207
Telephone: (800) 289-0963

Other distribution by:
Rockport Publishers, Inc.
Rockport, Massachusetts 01966-1299

ISBN 1-56496-192-3

10 9 8 7 6 5 4 3 2 1

Designer: Minnie Cho Design
Cover credits: See diagram below

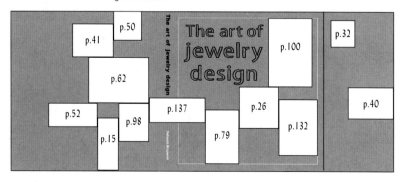

Printed in China

Acknowledgments

The Art of Jewelry Design offered me the opportunity to explore my field from a new perspective. Its completion would not have been possible without the generous help of friends and colleagues:

Boo Poulin first conceived of this book and initiated the project to recognize the accomplishments of production jewelry artists.

The community of artists who contributed to this book. They spoke candidly and insightfully about their work and their experiences in the field. They provided the excellent visual material for *The Art of Jewelry Design.*

My mother, Kay Whitcomb Keith, whose encouragement, interest, and enthusiasm has sustained me not only in this project, but in all my endeavors.

Marlene Ellin helped me to understand the dimensions of the project, explained a methodology to approach it, and patiently guided me through the publisher's contract.

Rebecca Brannon and Daniel Jocz shared their expertise and acumen in editing visual material.

Robert Weir provided me with computer and required software, and helped in so many ways large and small.

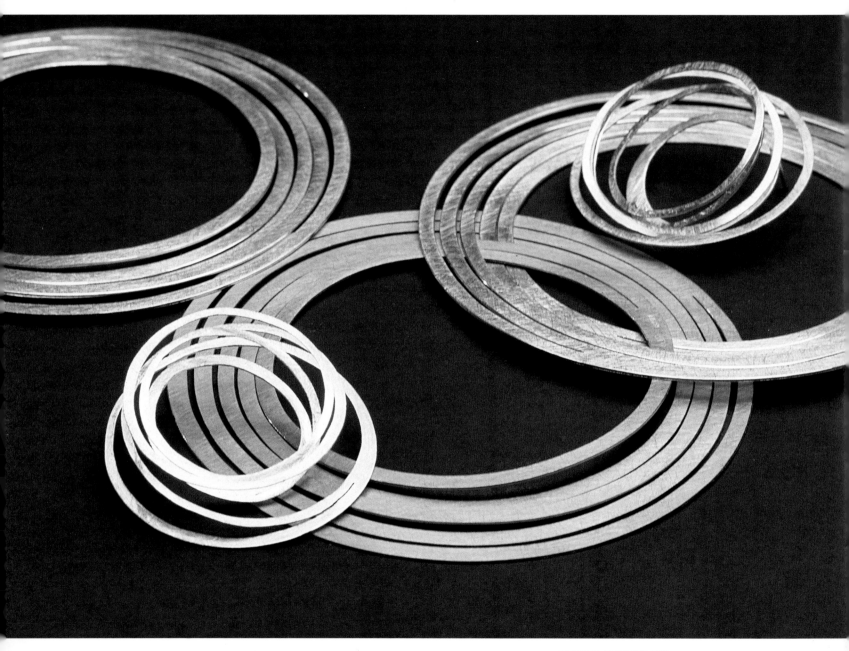

REIKO ISHIYAMA
BRACELETS AND EARRINGS
18-karat gold and sterling silver
Pierced and shaped

Photo: James Dee

Table of Contents

Introduction

To select the twenty artists presented in *The Art of Jewelry Design* was a daunting assignment. My first criterion was to create a balanced view of a vital and vibrant field. Happily, I was confronted by an embarrassment of riches—the field of talent is deep. The production jewelry created by these artists is informed by a unique approach to aesthetics, a strong sense of design, and an inventive attitude to technique and the possibilities of material—whether gold, silver, enamel, copper, aluminum, paper, or plastic.

Most of the artists featured in the book are grouped according to material: gold, silver, or more broadly, colored or alternative materials. Although this arrangement may seem arbitrary, certain design decisions naturally follow from the initial choice of material. For the jewelers working exclusively in gold, Heinrich and Good, and those working in silver, Suydam, Ishiyama, and Hamm, material contributes to the aesthetic quality and the perceived preciousness of their jewelry. Joan Parcher lets each of her materials—graphite, mica, or enamel—determine the ultimate form of her spirited jewelry. John Iversen has stated that all of his jewelry is about the secret which lies hidden in the materials he uses.

The jewelry presented in these pages is production work: intended to be made in multiples, according to market demand. However, it is never "commercial." What is the distinction? The object reveals the answer in its compelling connection to the hand of the artist. The commercial jewelry designer has little or no link to the manufacturing process, whether it is done by hand or by machine. Casting, die-forming, electroforming, and laser cutting are some of the production techniques

BARBARA HEINRICH
NECKLACE, EARRINGS, RINGS
18-karat gold, diamonds, mabe pearls, and
cultured pearls; Constructed and cast

used to reproduce forms. But each artist confesses to a surprising amount of handwork in forming processes, surface finishes, and in fitting and joining.

Concern with function, wearability, and quality characterize these artists' jewelry. There is an uninterrupted continuum from artist to jewelry to wearer. Commercial jewelry is "market-driven." Design decisions are based upon research oriented towards sales and marketing. Artists such as Boo Poulin and Thomas Mann, with their long-term commitment to experimental work, have patiently developed a market and a clientele for their jewelry.

The production jeweler is also a small business owner—and as such is responsive and susceptible to market forces. Responding to the economic decline of the early 1990s, Valerie Mitchell reduced the scale and proportions of her jewelry and began casting her pieces in brass and pewter. As the economy strengthens, she is once again doing more work in silver, and work that is larger in size and more ambitious in concept. During the same recession, necessity led David Urso to an intriguing invention: using aromatic herbs and spices to replace expensive color pigments in his inlaid epoxy jewelry.

Jewelry carries a precious weight beyond the value of materials, beyond the investment of time and skill, beyond the artist's intentions. It is the preciousness of celebration and of connection. Jewelry makes a visual connection, as well as an emotional, physical, and intellectual connection. The work in *The Art of Jewelry Design* transcends time and fashion and ensures that the jewelry will endure as artifacts and emblems to describe our culture to future generations.

Gold, the noble metal that can withstand time and the elements, has a long tradition in the history of jewelry. To continue, extend, and enrich the tradition and to become part of that history is a compelling impetus for the contemporary jeweler.

designing in gold

The physical properties of gold—its beauty, malleability, and preciousness— challenge the artist to create work that transcends fashion and trend. Each of the four artists in this chapter, working in a highly distinctive personal style, has accepted that challenge.

The preciousness of gold is a powerful metaphor for Barbara Heinrich and contributes to the spiritual dimension of her work. Her goldwork is distinguished by textures in which a softly glowing matte *skin* of 24-karat gold is illuminated by selective hand burnishing.

8

In her current goldwork, Kathe Timmerman retains the same playfulness and fluidity that characterized her colorful aluminum mesh jewelry. Although her palette has narrowed, Timmerman uses different surface finishes to describe her jewelry forms.

For Michael Good, gold is the perfect material—it is beautiful, malleable, and superbly suited to the specialized metalsmithing technique that yields his signature jewelry forms. He can work quite thin sheets of gold into hollow forms that have both strength and lightness. He polishes the gold to a high, reflective finish that also emphasizes his fluid design.

Gold is part of the palette of metals that Abrasha uses to construct his perfectly engineered forms. His jewelry is decidedly contemporary in its minimalist design and in its contrast of materials. Gold, brought to a softly brushed finish with burnished highlights, is the warm note among cool sterling silver, platinum, and stainless steel.

9

ABRASHA
NECKLACE
18-karat gold and diamonds
Fabricated

The immediate appeal of Barbara Heinrich's jewelry lies in the splendor of high-

karat gold and the seductive intimacy of textured surfaces. Her sense for pure

form—shown in the irregularly shaped discs of the Milky Way earrings, the

deftly chased surfaces of the Leaf group, and the gentle undulations of the

Barbara Heinrich

Ruffle series—has been described

as "casual perfection." She finds

form and surface, material and

technique to be inseparable, and she often spends as much time creating the

texture of a distinctive surface as she does fabricating the form. The gold

surface is very important—"it is sensitive and responsive, like a person's skin."

The noble yet malleable qualities of gold serve as powerful metaphors for

Heinrich; she believes that such qualities also lie within each person.

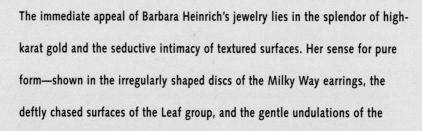

Heinrich's jewelry joins the jewelry-making traditions of two countries. By the time she came to the United States to study, she had been formally apprenticed to a goldsmith in Germany for three years and had studied at the Fachhoch-schule für Gestaltung in Pforzheim. In the graduate metals program at Rochester Institute of Technology, Heinrich took an experimental approach to material (working with aluminum and plastic) and to design (concentrating on personal expression).

When she set up her studio, Heinrich combined the two educational experiences. Disciplined technique and creative design allow her complete freedom to express her artistic vision in gold. She seeks to create timeless classics whose aesthetic qualities endure just as gold does.

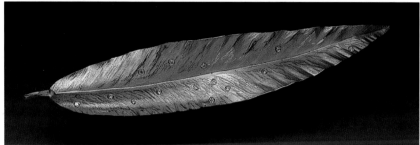

BROOCH *Leaf*
18-karat gold and diamonds
Hammer-textured and formed

11

NECKLACE *Leaf*
18-karat gold and sterling silver
Forged and constructed

Specific inspirations are often the impulse for a new body of work. Fairy tales,

painting, forms found in nature, music, prayer, or simply daydreaming—

anything that touches me deeply—can set off the creative process. I prepare

myself by keeping a sketchbook at hand.

The Ruffle series started with the underlying image of a flower opening

up. In some of my earlier jewelry, such as the Milky Way group, the reference

technique was clear. Now I do not want the design to be too narrative or

too specific. I want to capture the substance of the inspiration,

the beauty of the image—but the form must speak on its own.

After developing a clear idea of what I want the piece to look like, I then

consider the most direct way to make it. I develop forming and texturing

techniques to suit the design and the material. The Ruffle

Pendant is fabricated in 18-karat red gold, quite a

hard alloy, that comes from Germany. I roll the

RING   *Diamond*
18-karat gold and diamonds
Constructed

metal between sheets of paper to give it a matte surface. I like to make the jewelry the way I draw it; thus, when I saw out the disc shape, I do not want a perfect circle. I hammer the edges to thicken them, and then dome the discs in a wood dapping block with wood punches. The gold is thin enough to "ruffle" with forming pliers, but still thick enough to resist warping. I repeat the process of bending with pliers and gently flattening the disc several times, until the ruffles form a casual, random pattern. I nest the two cups and solder them together, and then solder a short stem of twisted gold wire to the center.

I finish the surface with powdered pumice, applied with a toothbrush and water. I heat the gold gently with the torch and pickle it in acid, a technique called depletion gilding, to create a layer of fine gold. I contrast the soft, warm glow of this matte surface with the hard shine of the hand-burnished edge. This selective highlighting illuminates the surface and defines the form. Finally, I epoxy a freshwater pearl to the wire stem, and the pendant is complete.

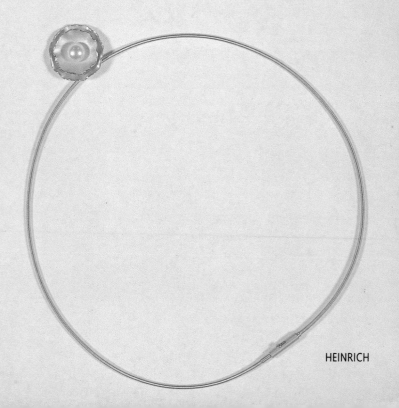

HEINRICH

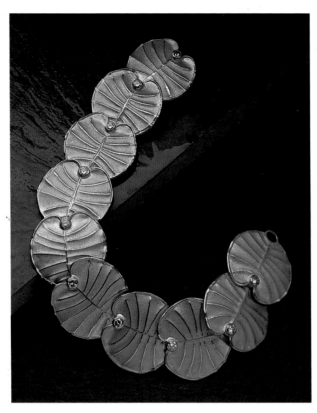

14

BRACELET *Leaf*
18-karat gold and diamonds
Chased and constructed

BROOCHES
18-karat gold and opal
Hammer-textured and constructed

barbara heinrich

EARRINGS, PENDANT, BROOCH, RING
Ruffle Group
18-karat gold and freshwater pearls
Constructed

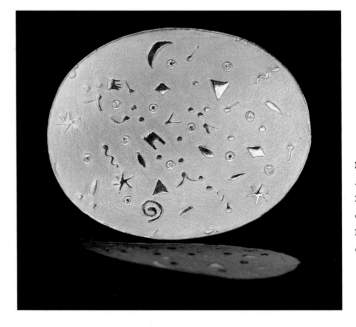

BROOCH
Milky Way
18-karat gold
and diamonds
Embossed
and constructed

BROOCH AND EARRINGS
18-karat gold and tourmaline cabochons
Hammer-textured and forged

BROOCH　　*Opal*
18-karat gold and boulder opal
Hammer-textured and constructed

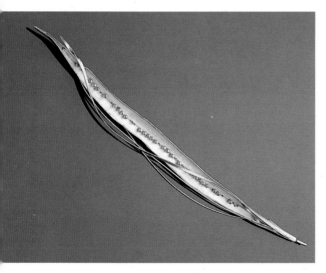

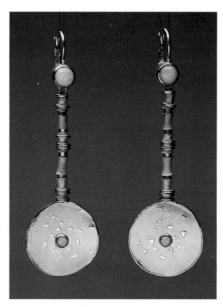

PIN
18-karat gold, sterling silver, and cultured
gray pearls
Forged and constructed

EARRINGS　　*Milky Way*
18-karat gold and opals
Embossed, forged, and constructed

RINGS
18-karat gold, colored sapphires,
diamonds, and pearl
Textured and constructed

An interest in women's experience and history, particularly the image of women in nineteenth-century novels and in contemporary fashion, informs Kathe Timmerman's approach to jewelry design. She journeyed through Australia, Asia, the Middle East, and Europe before entering the metal-

Kathe Timmerman

smithing program at San Diego State University. Whimsical forged jewelry and raised sculptural vessels formed the focus of her student work.

Timmerman introduced a collection of aluminum mesh jewelry in her first production line. The fine-gauge screen, anodized to brilliant hues, captured silver and gold foil in its grid. The mesh, recalling the transparency of lingerie, formed easily. The color-and-texture collage

compositions, inspired by the work of
Jean Arp, were framed in silver, which
provided structural support for the mesh.
The relatively low cost
of the material allowed
Timmerman to play.

Her collection has
grown in new directions,
adding silver and gold earrings, rings, and bracelets
in simple sculpted forms. Timmerman's
sense of fun shows in the way that rings and
bracelets wrap informally around the finger
or wrist, gracefully enhancing the natural
contours of the body.

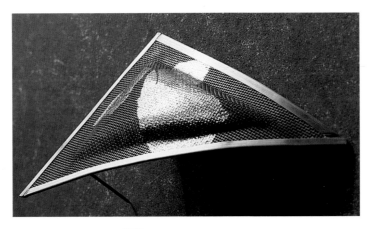

PIN
Aluminum mesh with gold, silver,
and copper foils, and sterling silver
Anodized and die-formed

17

EARRINGS   *Magic Carpet Ride*
Sterling silver, 24-karat vermeil, aluminum mesh
with gold, silver, and copper foils, and pearls
Formed and fabricated

18

Recently I have designed a line of gold jewelry with the goal of making it as playful as my work in mesh. As these designs have become more fluid and more sophisticated, I have refined my technique. I shape the abstract forms to suggest exotic flowers, such as orchids.

Though I like to work with Ceylon sapphires and black pearls, metal is always primary. I form it to embrace the stone, which provides color and contrasts with the gold. I sometimes combine different surface finishes—the matte surface of glass-bead-blasted gold with the reflective finish of tumbled gold—to complement the convex and concave shapes in

technique

the jewelry. Often, I construct paper models from my sketches before working the metal. But if the mental image is clear enough, I work with the metal

EARRINGS
18-karat yellow and 14-karat
white gold, and diamonds
Forged

immediately. I use both production techniques (including die-forming) and labor-intensive hand-forming techniques (such as working with a mallet over small anvil heads and forming blocks).

Whereas mesh only suggested the possibility of sculptural form, the work in silver and gold is more three-dimensional, more fully realized, and more resolved. The natural environment of the seashore and the voluptuous forms of the female and the flower inspire my design.

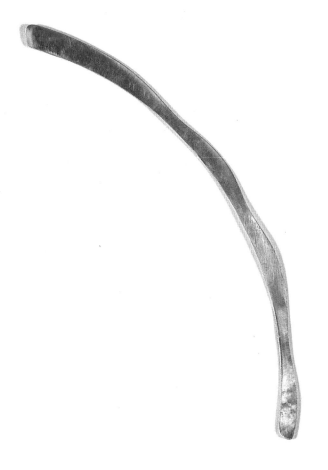

19

EARRINGS *Mesh*
Sterling silver and 24-karat vermeil
Formed

EARRINGS *Spiral*
Aluminum mesh with gold and copper foils, and sterling silver
Anodized

kathe timmerman

EARRINGS
18-karat gold
Forged

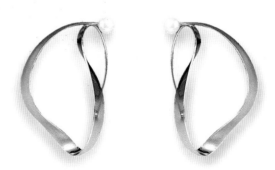

EARRINGS
Sterling silver and 24-karat vermeil
Formed and forged

STICKPINS
Gold, sterling silver, and ivory
Forged and fabricated

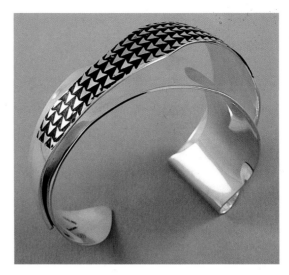

BRACELET
Sterling silver and copper
Formed and photo-etched

RING AND EARRINGS
14-karat and 18-karat gold, 24-karat vermeil, and sapphire
Formed and forged

PENDANT
18-karat yellow gold and 14-karat white gold,
and Australian opal
Forged

Self-taught jeweler Michael Good started working in 1968. His first designs

were simple flat shapes with hammered surfaces, cut from thin sheets of

14-karat gold. Then he began to experiment with ways to make the gold

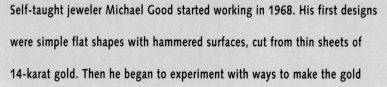 sheet three-dimensional by

hammering the material into

hollow forms. But it was not

until he was introduced to the work of the influential teacher and metalsmith

Heikki Seppä, with his new approach to hammer raising, that Good had

the technical means to realize his vision of a fluid, dynamic line moving

gracefully through space.

Good found the perfect union of concept and technology. He could hammer and form his flat metal pattern with a cross peen hammer over specially designed sinusoidal stakes, using Seppä's anticlastic raising technique, to create hollow "shell" forms. Within his design vocabulary, any form was now theoretically possible.

Good reinterpreted and refined Seppä's ideas for the scale of jewelry. The success of Good's signature jewelry forms relies on his ability to "move" metal. That is, working with hammer and stake to finesse the flat sheet into a stable, hollow, three-dimensional structure.

RINGS
Knot, HPE, and Double Loop©
18-karat yellow gold
Anticlastic raised

23

PENDANT
Spirit Sun Pendant with Spirit Sun Diamond©
18-karat yellow gold and diamond
Anticlastic raised

24

technique

My designs are directly related to the material and the technique I use. The anticlastic forming process determines the aesthetics of the piece. It takes away all the extraneous things; there is no soldering, no clasps.

Each piece begins with a sheet of 18-karat gold, on which the pattern is drawn. For each new design, a flat pattern is developed, then hammered into an anticlastic form. I alter the flat pattern until I finally reach the three dimensional form as I want it to be. Making the prototype is the most exciting part. That is the heart of it.

To take the flat sheet to a dimensional, hollow structure involves forming the metal. The shape of the tool determines the shape of the finished piece.

PENDANT
18-karat yellow gold
Anticlastic raised

I hammer the flat, gold pattern on a sinusoidal stake of steel or plastic until the piece acquires the characteristic curved shell structure. At this point, the partially formed anticlastic strip has great structural strength, but it can still move freely about its axis and can be twisted easily in both directions. I systematically bend and twist the partially formed strip so that it can be turned in just about any direction. The concave side of the anticlast will always remain on the outside of the curve, adding strength and definition to the forms. When I have chosen a particular form, usually after the first course of raising, I continue hammering the piece until the final shape is obtained. I close in the form with a smooth-edged uniform seam that runs symmetrically along it.

BRACELET　　*Knot©*
18-karat yellow gold
Anticlastic raised

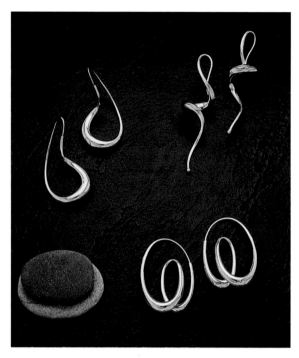

EARRINGS　　*Figure Eight, Helicoidal, and Baroque©*
18-karat yellow gold
Anticlastic raised

BRACELET AND EARRINGS　　*Ruffle©*
18-karat yellow gold
Anticlastic raised

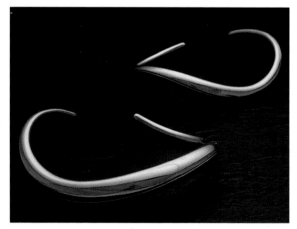

BRACELETS　　*Light and Heavy Wave Cuff©*
18-karat yellow gold
Anticlastic raised

BRACELET *Double Loop*©
18-karat yellow gold
Anticlastic raised

EARRINGS *Single Loop*©
18-karat yellow gold
Anticlastic raised

27

PENDANT AND EARRINGS *Zahna*©
18-karat yellow gold
Anticlastic raised

michael good

BRACELET
Triple Loop with Diamonds©
18-karat yellow gold and diamonds
Anticlastic raised

EARRINGS
Platinum Rolled Torque©
18-karat yellow gold
and platinum
Anticlastic raised

Austere, restrained, intellectual **are words that describe the jewelry of Abrasha. No decorative details detract from the pristine geometric composition.**

Abrasha

Yet this engineered perfection and sense of order reveal the unexpected: the contrast of materials, the logic of asymmetry.

Abrasha's decision to become a goldsmith was instantaneous. Visiting a jeweler's studio in his native Amsterdam, he was captivated by the tools and the mystique of the workshop. Convinced of his métier, he entered the Goldschmiedschule in Pforzheim, the historic center of the German jewelry industry.

Abrasha's apprenticeship as a model maker in a jewelry company introduced him to some of Germany's most influential innovators in design. He later worked as an assistant to the master goldsmith Klaus Ullrich. By the mid-1970s, Abrasha had arrived in San Francisco. He did bench work and eventually set up his own workshop. Gradually he began to execute his own designs and to develop his distinctive formal vocabulary.

Abrasha describes his design as industrial, cool, machinelike. His signature rivets, which connect materials that cannot be joined by soldering, fulfill the Bauhaus principle that form should follow function. Abrasha's jewelry forms—circles, spheres, and cones, punctuated by gold rivets, brilliant diamonds, or crisp edges—appeal to logic and reason. The rigidly

RING
18-karat gold, platinum,
and diamond
Fabricated

geometric square pin series explores material within clearly delineated design parameters.

Abrasha's jewelry speaks of discipline and control. Although the forms may seem cerebral, even cool, the beautiful and unexpected surfaces betray the hand of a sensitive artist. Rewarding close attention, his work yields the exquisite detail, the subtle refinement.

29

BRACELET
24-karat and 18-karat gold, stainless steel, and diamond
Machined and fabricated

30

The Bauhaus aesthetic, the Russian constructivists, and Japanese design sensibilities influence my work. The design process starts with an idea, then a quick sketch. My concern for precision, geometry, and balance leads to many possible variations of the original idea before I arrive at its final expression. For me, the design process had always been laborious and time-consuming: my German training dictated that I draw with ballpoint pen, with no erasures. Now, after the initial drawing, I move to the computer to quickly generate variations of measurement, scale, and proportion.

The finished drawing serves as a guideline for making the piece. During the working process, I make decisions at each step, thus refining the concept. I work in a restrained palette of materials: 18-karat and 24-karat gold, sterling silver, platinum, stainless steel, and diamonds. I am drawn to the rich yellow color of gold. **technique**

**CUFFLINKS
AND TUXEDO STUDS**
18-karat gold
and diamonds
Fabricated

Silver, oxidized to a dark black, creates a wonderful foil

for high-karat golds; the cold reflectivity of polished

platinum provides a subtle contrast to round or square-cut

diamonds; and stainless steel introduces an industrial,

contemporary element.

By inclination and by training,

I am a fabricator. I alloy 18-karat

gold to make both sheet and wire

by weighing out pure gold, fine silver,

and copper, melting them in a crucible

with my torch, and then pouring the molten metal into

an ingot mold. I forge the billet and roll it to the desired

thickness. I then lay out my design on the sheet gold,

sawing and filing shapes almost to size. I use pliers,

hammers, bending tools, punches, and doming blocks to

achieve dimensional forms. I file the individual pieces yet

again to exact measurement, and then fit parts together

and solder them. If stainless steel is included, I drill

holes for the rivets. I then set the stones and bring the

surface to a soft, brushed finish, burnishing the edges

and bezels. Then, finally, I join the stainless steel with

24-karat gold rivets.

31

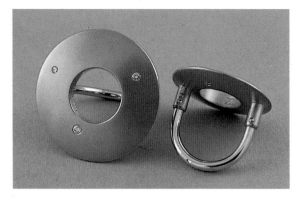

RINGS
18-karat gold, platinum, and diamonds
Fabricated

RING
18-karat gold,
platinum,
and diamonds
Fabricated

32

PENDANT
18-karat gold and diamonds
Fabricated

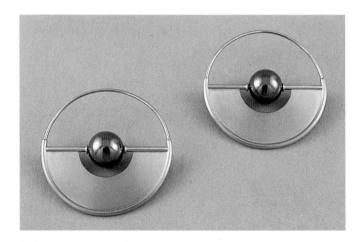

EARRINGS
18-karat gold, stainless steel, and hematite
Fabricated

EARRINGS
18-karat gold,
stainless steel,
and hematite
Fabricated

BRACELET
Stainless steel and 18-karat gold
Fabricated and cast

RING
18-karat gold
and stainless steel
Cast and fabricated

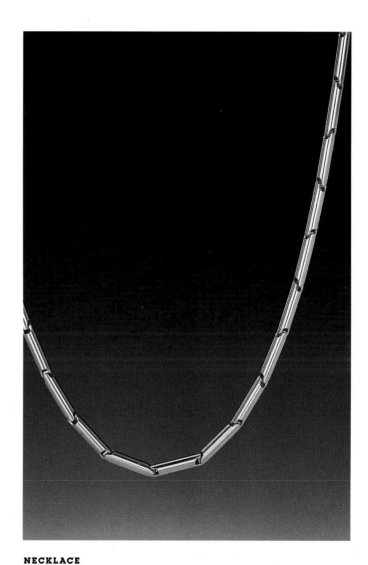

NECKLACE
Stainless steel and 18-karat gold
Machined, cast, and fabricated

PINS   #5 and #6
Stainless steel, plywood, 18-karat gold, and sterling silver
Fabricated

33

Although a highly-developed personal aesthetic is evident in each of their jewelry, Reiko Ishiyama, Didi Suydam, and

designing in silver

Lorelei Hamm find common ground in their material of choice—silver. And, surprisingly, silver contributes to the artist's shared sculptural aesthetic, one that embraces both the organic and the geometric, and emphasizes structure and three-dimensional form.

Each artist uses traditional metalsmithing techniques to fabricate her jewelry. Both Suydam and Hamm's architectonic forms are hollow constructed, but Suydam replicates her prototypes by casting multiples, and Hamm

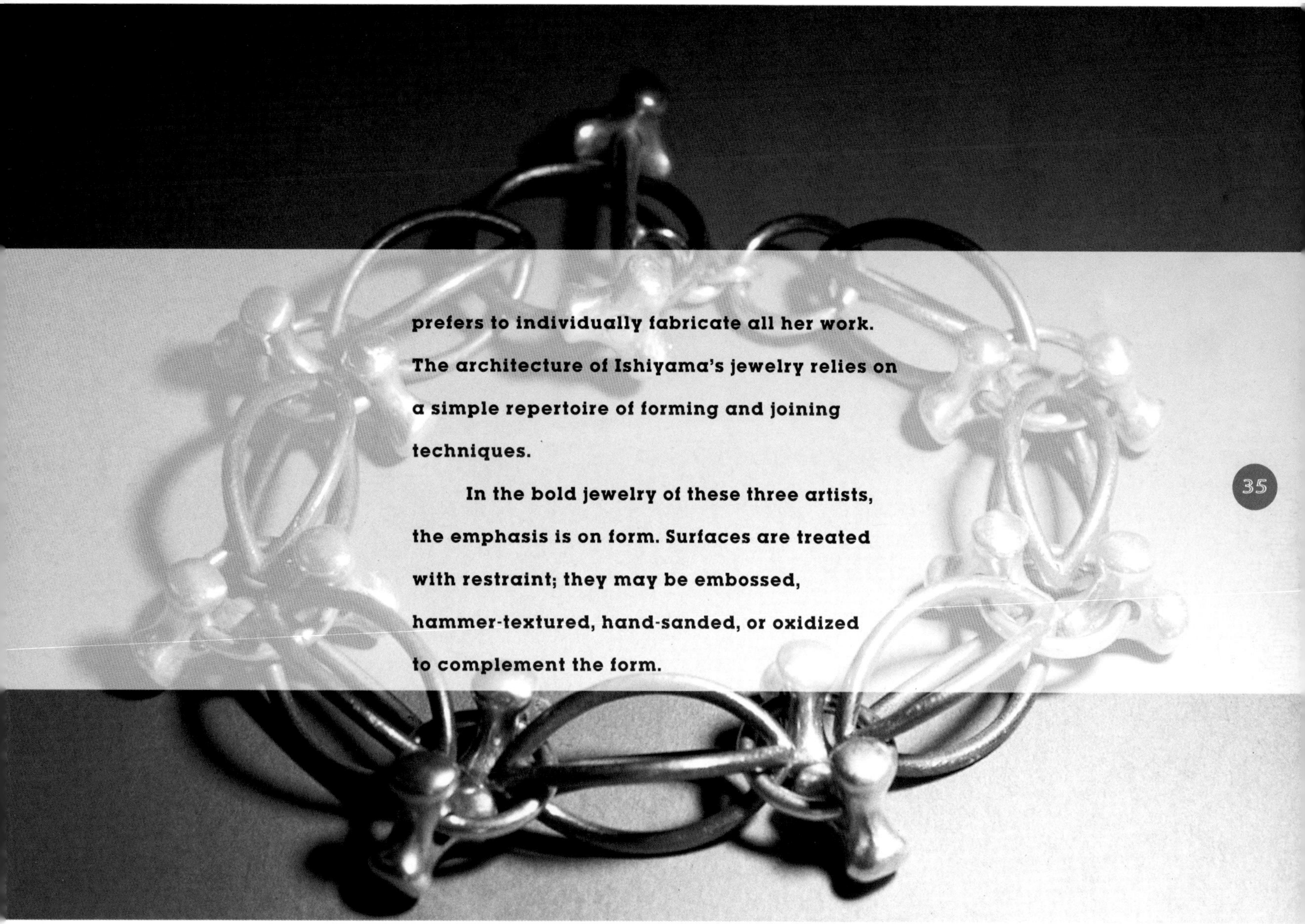

prefers to individually fabricate all her work.
The architecture of Ishiyama's jewelry relies on
a simple repertoire of forming and joining
techniques.

In the bold jewelry of these three artists,
the emphasis is on form. Surfaces are treated
with restraint; they may be embossed,
hammer-textured, hand-sanded, or oxidized
to complement the form.

35

LORELEI HAMM
BRACELET
Sterling silver
Cast and fabricated

Reiko Ishiyama remembers, as a young woman, watching a Japanese metalsmith forge a simple tool. She was fascinated that metal, which had always seemed so hard, could be soft and malleable. That private epiphany determined her course.

She became apprenticed to a metalsmith who specialized in objects for the Japanese tea

Reiko Ishiyama

ceremony. Eventually she moved into sculpture, working with welded copper, iron, and steel. Although conceptual art was popular in Japan in the late 1960s and 1970s, Ishiyama remained fascinated by the material—how it could be transformed in the artist's hands.

When she first arrived in New York in the mid-1980s, both her work space and range of tools were very limited. Working with only a jeweler's sawframe on a small tabletop, Ishiyama produced a collection of jewelry of remarkable freshness and spontaneity.

Architectural spaces, and the play of light and shadow they create, have inspired her design. In her earlier work, Ishiyama presented a form, sawed a path that followed its contour, and then gently pulled the flat shape into a three-dimensional shape. The pattern of light and shadow of such a piece has as strong a presence as the object itself. In her current bracelets, thin, narrow, undulating strips of metal recall the materials and techniques of basketry.

Ishiyama does not seek to completely control the metal, but rather to understand its qualities and possibilities. In both the organic and the geometric forms, the artist's sense of touch is expressed through the softly textured surfaces, the crisp yet wavy edges, and the interesting dimensional quality of her pieces. Without dominating or overpowering the wearer, Ishiyama's jewelry has a strong aesthetic presence.

PINS
Sterling silver
Pierced and shaped; sandblasted finish

37

BRACELETS
Sterling silver and gold plate
Pierced and shaped

Photography: James Dee

I don't usually begin by drawing or sketching, but rather by bending, shaping, hammering, or cutting pieces of silver. My designs evolve through working

technique

directly with the material. My hands are the ultimate source of my ideas—I develop a design and streamline the technical process through this way of working. Good pieces are a duet of material and technique: both are equally important for a design to be successful.

I use the jeweler's traditional tools and techniques (hammering, sawing, filing, and soldering) to achieve form. I choose surface textures to describe the form: silver might be sandblasted, hammered into a plate of pitted iron, or hand-finished with coarse sandpaper.

I work exclusively with silver and gold. The way silver reflects or absorbs light, depending upon its finish, captivates me; I also like how it ages, developing a

PINS
Sterling silver
Hammer-textured and shaped
Photo: James Dee

natural patina reflecting wear or exposure to the

elements. Although my jewelry is often intricate and

delicate, each structure is strong. The sterling

silver comes from Japan, manufactured to

achieve a consistent temper. Because I

use a hammer to texture it, the metal

becomes work-hardened before the

forming processes begin. Designing one-of-

a-kind pieces offers opportunities for artistic

growth, strengthening my senses, pushing me in

new directions, and allowing me to capture glimmers

and flashes of new ideas. And these

ideas, simplified in design and

technique, inspire the signature

production jewelry

that I also create.

ISHIYAMA

EARRINGS
18-karat gold
Hammer-textured and formed

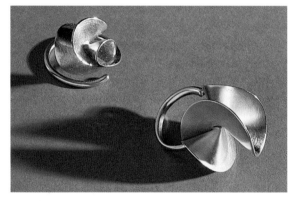

RINGS
Sterling silver and gold plate
Fabricated

PINS
Sterling silver and gold plate
Pierced and shaped

BRACELETS
Sterling silver
Hammer-textured and constructed

EARRINGS
Sterling silver and gold plate
Hammer-textured and formed

Photography: James Dee

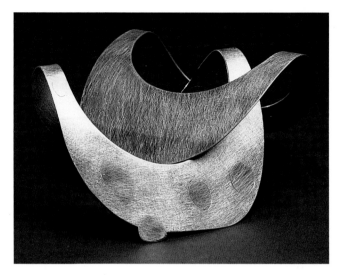

BRACELETS
14-karat gold, sterling silver, and gold plate
Pierced, laminated, and formed

BRACELETS
Sterling silver and gold plate
Pierced and shaped

reiko ishiyama

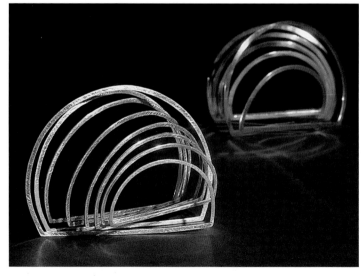

BRACELETS
Sterling silver
Hammered and formed

EARRINGS
Sterling silver
Pierced and shaped; sandblasted finish

Didi Suydam entered Rhode Island School of Design intending to study sculpture. Although she soon switched to jewelry design, sculptural concerns continue to influence her work. Suydam interprets the body as landscape, and her jewelry as site-specific. Her bracelets,

Didi Suydam

earrings, and necklaces are meant to move, to sway, and to be felt, physically and visually. Her work harmonizes with the natural rhythms and contours of the body.

A semester spent studying in Rome had a profound impact on Suydam. Her jewelry resonates with associations to ancient artifacts, architectural and natural forms, and formal geometry.

Although Suydam makes a clear distinction between her impressive one-of-a-kind jewelry and her elegant production jewelry, they share a common aesthetic and sense of form. She makes a lot of drawings to establish her forms. Then she simplifies them, reconfiguring proportion, rhythm, and repetition. She must visualize shapes: how they work together, how to construct them, and how to make them function as jewelry. She finds the problem-solving nature of production design both challenging and satisfying.

BRACELET
Sterling silver and commercial chain
Cast and textured

EARRINGS
Sterling silver and gold plate
Cast, textured, and oxidized

PENDANTS   *Vessel*
Sterling silver, gold plate, and commercial chain
Cast and oxidized

43

Silver suits the proportion and scale of my jewelry. To achieve dimensional form, I fabricate the metal, using traditional hollow construction techniques: scoring and folding, and forming with hammers, stakes, and small dapping punches. In designing for production, I seek solutions, not compromises. How can I make a piece as quickly and simply as possible?

technique

Casting offers a way to reproduce three-dimensional forms, and the result can actually be a technical and aesthetic improvement

over the hand-fabricated prototype. I always cast the form hollow and then solder on a back plate—I want the piece to be "whole," yet light in weight.

Sometimes I emboss the surface of the fabricated prototype to create a relief texture; that surface is replicated in the cast form. Or I may apply a wire-brushed finish to the completed casting. My more recent designs rely on

44

EARRINGS
Jester series
Sterling silver
Cast with hand-sanded
satin finish

labor-intensive hand-sanded finishes to complement the form.

I have always liked the look of hand-forged links, so I use my

own cast hammered   links as well as commercial chain.

Chains are important   visual, functional, and

metaphorical elements in   my jewelry.

Sinuous and textural, the chain connects separate

parts to create a whole, as it

allows those parts to move

interdependently. My personal

experience often finds formal

expression in my jewelry. As I now balance the joys and

demands of motherhood with those of the studio,

my vocabulary of forms has evolved. Shapes have become

softer, more   organic, more sensuous.

Connections   between forms create a seamless

structural unity. Each element is crucial to the whole.

45

SUYDAM

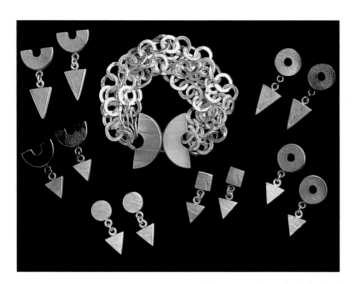

EARRINGS AND BRACELET
Sterling silver and gold plate
Cast, textured, and oxidized

EARRINGS, BRACELETS, AND PENDANT
Sterling silver, gold plate, and commercial chain
Cast and oxidized

46

didi suydam

BRACELET   *Jester series: Roller*
Sterling silver
Cast with hand-sanded satin finish

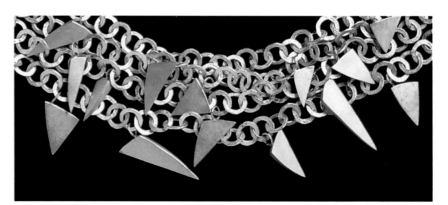

NECKLACE   *Free-Form series*
Sterling silver and gold plate

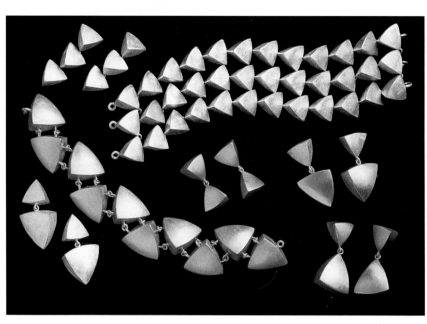

EARRINGS AND BRACELETS

Free-Form series: Earrings, Armadillo Bracelet, and Fat-Form Bracelet

Sterling silver and gold plate

Cast with hand-sanded satin finish

NECKLACE
Pod series
Sterling silver
and gold plate
Cast

47

EARRINGS AND BRACELETS   *Jester series*
Sterling silver and gold plate
Cast

EARRINGS   *Medieval Chandelier series*
Sterling silver, gold plate, and commercial chain
Cast and oxidized

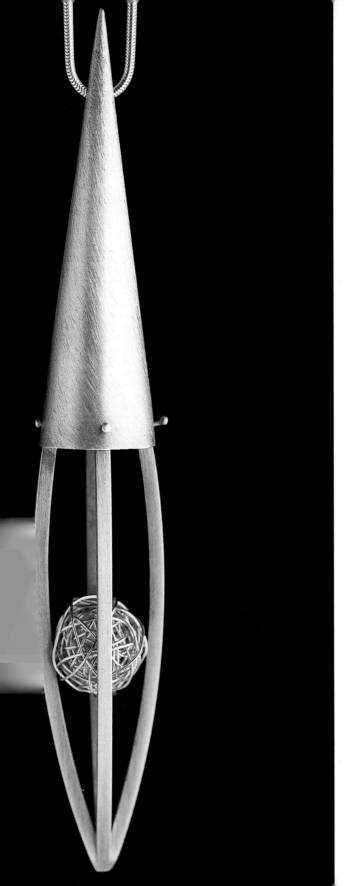

Architecture, industrial forms, and organic shapes influence Lorelei Hamm's jewelry design. In her early work she combined alternative materials such as rubber and silk-screened acrylic with traditional sterling silver and space-age niobium in designs for hard-edged, geometric jewelry. Using the refractive metal niobium, which is inherently light in weight, malleable, and easy to anodize, Hamm explored color and scale in her fibula pins and earrings.

Since 1981, Hamm has designed production and one-of-a-kind jewelry, as well as tables and tabletop objects. Her work has evolved in design, technique, and material. She now works almost exclusively in hollow forms made of sterling silver, exploring its tonal possibilities by texturing it, oxidizing it,

Lorelei Hamm

or contrasting it with gold or copper. Organic shapes juxtaposed with industrial structures are a recurring theme in her work. She favors formal circles and ovals, using sheet silver to create pointed, elongated ovoid forms or, most recently, the architectonics of her cone variations.

Hamm contrasts solid geometric shapes with linear patterns. She often places tangled balls of wire or elegant wire networks within a solid structure. Her recent bracelets, among her most satisfying work, continue this investigation of line. Industrial in design, each piece combines rhythm, proportion, movement, and stasis in an integrated structure.

Hamm defines jewelry as the intimate bond between the object of adornment and the wearer. Her jewelry projects an aura of mystery, suggesting powerful amulets, artifacts of an industrial age.

NECKLACE
Sterling silver and copper
Hollow constructed

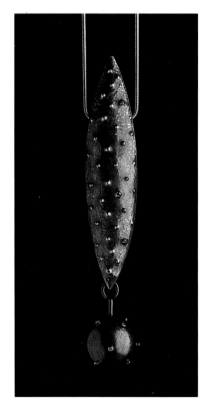

NECKLACE
Sterling silver
Hollow formed
and constructed

49

NECKLACE
14-karat gold and sterling silver
Fabricated and hollow formed

technique

In the past, my forms, joined using cold connection techniques, were primarily geometric and hard-edged. Inspired by themes of technology and industry, I incorporated many different materials—plastics, rubber, niobium—into each piece.

Today, I work with traditional metals and traditional techniques. I do not use stones or chemical patination, but rather the monotone hues that metal produces naturally. My imagery now is drawn from personal experience. I want to create a visual language for jewelry based on the organic, industrial, and cultural symbols that influence us all. For example, scars or suture marks, symbols of the pain and growth

PIN
18-karat gold and sterling silver
Fabricated

inherent in life, have become part of my
dialogue and indicate the direction of my work
to come.

I work with sterling silver, sometimes incorporating
18-karat gold or copper. I use hollow construction and
hollow forming techniques, fabrication, and casting to create
these pieces. Ninety-five per cent of my tools are hand
tools—I like the control of handworking each part of a piece
and prefer textures that can only be created by hand.
No two pieces ever look exactly the same.

HAMM

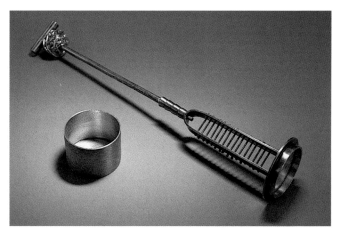

RING BOX
14-karat gold and sterling silver
Constructed and fabricated

NECKLACE
14-karat gold and sterling silver
Hollow formed and fabricated

52

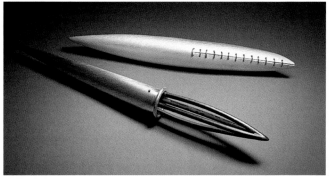

PINS
18-karat gold, fine silver, and sterling silver
Hollow formed and fabricated

NECKLACE
18-karat and 14-karat gold and sterling silver
Hollow formed and fabricated

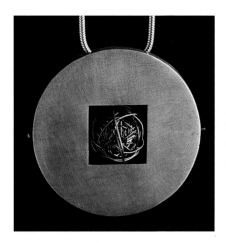

NECKLACE
18-karat gold and
sterling silver
Hollow constructed

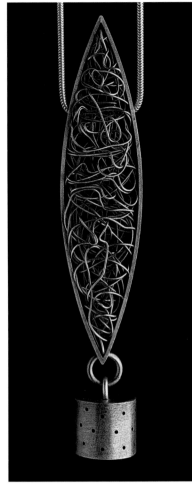

NECKLACE
Sterling silver
Fabricated and
hollow constructed

EARRINGS
Sterling silver
Cast and fabricated

lorelei hamm

53

BRACELETS
Sterling silver and bronze
Cast and fabricated

BRACELET
18-karat and 14-karat gold and sterling silver
Cast, hollow constructed, and fabricated

These five colorists present new ways to think about the
relationship of jewelry structure to surface, color, and
material.

Ginny Whitney, Mary Kanda, and David Urso house
their painterly color compositions in metal frames.
Whitney captures the time-honored tradition of enameling
in canvases that are scaled and proportioned to the
human body. When Kanda decided to create mosaic
jewelry, her experiments eventually led her to the colorful

designing with color

seed beads that
she had been
collecting for years. These beads, with their ethnic and
tribal associations, satisfied her technical requirements

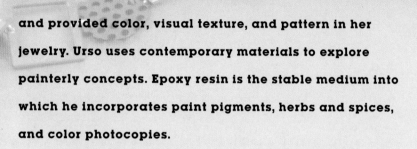

and provided color, visual texture, and pattern in her jewelry. Urso uses contemporary materials to explore painterly concepts. Epoxy resin is the stable medium into which he incorporates paint pigments, herbs and spices, and color photocopies.

John Iversen, well-known for his carved enamel brooches and bracelets, uses patination to chemically color the metal in the Basket and the Leaf series. Surface, structure, and color are coherently united in the material. In the same way, Peggy Eng integrates unexpected forms and vibrant colors in her anodized aluminum jewelry.

55

PEGGY ENG
NECKPIECE *Whimsy*
Aluminum
Textured, anodized, and dyed

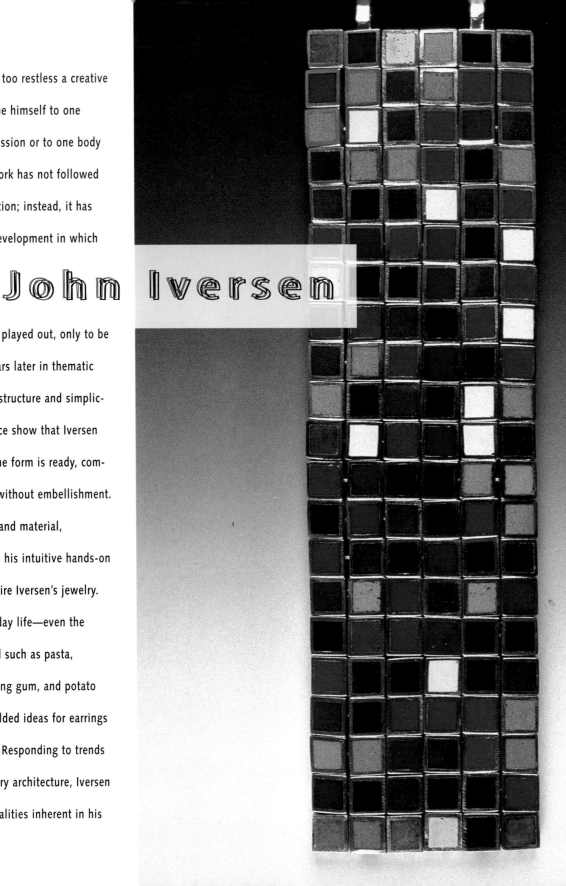

John Iversen is too restless a creative talent to confine himself to one means of expression or to one body of work. His work has not followed a simple evolution; instead, it has undergone a development in which themes are introduced,

John Iversen

expanded, and played out, only to be returned to years later in thematic variation. The structure and simplicity of each piece show that Iversen knows when the form is ready, complete in itself without embellishment.

Process and material, combined with his intuitive hands-on approach, inspire Iversen's jewelry. So does everyday life—even the shapes of food such as pasta, Chiclets chewing gum, and potato chips have yielded ideas for earrings and brooches. Responding to trends in contemporary architecture, Iversen reveals the qualities inherent in his materials, paying particular attention to surfaces and finishes. He explores the possibilities for color and texture in each material, discovering another way of bending or stretching it, or a new finish.

Iversen combines the Old World tradition of fine goldsmithing with New World artistic liberty. His family roots are in Germany, which he left at age seventeen to enter a four-year apprenticeship in goldsmithing in Vancouver, Canada. He returned to Germany as an independent student at Hanau's famed Staatliche Zeichen Academy. Taking courses in basic design, enameling, and silversmithing, Iversen continued his technical training as he developed his creative voice. In the late 1970s he moved to New York City, initially designing for industry.

Iversen works with enamel, precious metals, pearls, bronze, and iron. Though he uses both casting and construction to create his works, he sometimes steps outside the canon of conventional jewelry-making techniques. The web structure of the Basket series demands dexterity with needle and thread. Iversen draws on a remarkable repertoire of skills to achieve his jewelry forms.

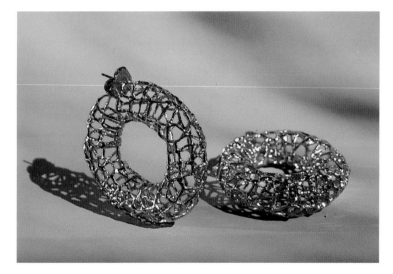

EARRINGS   *Circle Basket*
14-karat gold and sterling silver
Sewn, cast, constructed, and plated

BRACELET   *Multicolored Enamel*
24-karat gold, sterling silver, copper, and enamel
Cast and constructed

To make beautiful and expressive work, my approach is the same, whether I am designing a one-of-a-kind piece or a production piece of jewelry. What distinguishes the production work is that the basic form can be reproduced. Then a lot of complex and intricate handwork goes into completing the piece.

The actual concept for a new idea occurs in a split second. I draw a lot, which only leads to more ambivalence about the initial design. It's at the workbench, experimenting with material and manufacture, where the idea takes shape.

technique

The joy of designing comes from working out the technicalities of how a piece is put together or how to actually make something I visualized. I usually start a body of work very unconsciously with a very rough piece. It is just the spontaneous expression that matters.

BRACELET *Tower* (detail)
24-karat gold and sterling silver
Cast, constructed, and plated

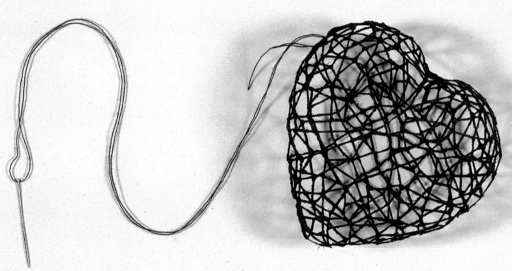

I have been sewing since my early childhood, whether it was new clothes for my teddy bear or riggings on sailing ships. This is the kernel that years later developed into the Basket series: using needle and thread to create webbed patterns of gold. Each piece starts with a shape—a shell or a pebble, for example—that I wrap in nonstick foil, plastic, or wax paper. I sew a web pattern onto the form with nylon string, then apply glue to harden the string and to make it rigid. I cut the webbed structure apart so that the core can be removed, and fuse it back together with a hot wax tool. I coat the string with wax to the desired thickness, then cast it using the lost wax technique. The finished piece may be a pendant, a bracelet, or a brooch.

59

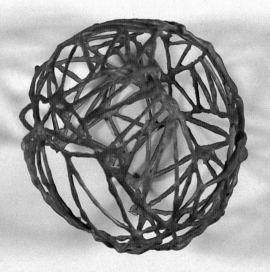

IVERSEN

PENDANT *Small Basket*
24-karat gold and sterling silver
Sewn, cast, constructed, and gold-plated

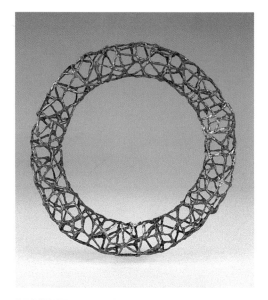

BRACELET *Basket*
18-karat gold and sterling silver
Sewn, cast, and constructed

60

PINS *Bronze Leaf series*
Sterling silver, bronze, and nickel silver
Cast, constructed, and oxidized

NECKLACE *Seed*
Sterling silver
Constructed and plated

EARRINGS   *Spike Wing*
24-karat gold and sterling silver
Cast and plated

john iversen

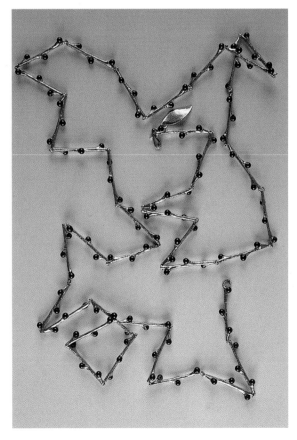

EARRINGS   *Long Swirl*
24-karat and 14-karat gold
and sterling silver
Cast and constructed

BRACELET   *Tower*
24-karat gold and sterling silver
Cast, constructed, and plated

NECKLACE   *Willow*
18-karat gold and black pearls
Cast, constructed, and plated

Peggy Eng's work is defined by her choice of material—aluminum—and she

exploits its potential for color, texture, and form to the fullest.

Eng majored in jewelry and metalsmithing as an undergraduate, then

continued graduate work at the Appalachian Center for Crafts in Tennessee.

She established her jewelry design studio in 1986, making both production

and one-of-a-kind pieces. Eng's first production line featured precolored

Peggy Eng

aluminum, a

material that

attracted her because of its color—but it proved limiting. By anodizing and

coloring aluminum herself, Eng has realized more sophisticated designs

and achieved greater control of the material. She can use a wide range of

forms and extrusions of lightweight aluminum, and her palette has

expanded to gloriously rich, saturated color that spans the color spectrum.

As her work has grown, Eng's designs have become more spare. She achieves a strong visual impact by taking a minimalist approach, simplifying each design to its essence. She strives to create wearable jewelry, eliminating unnecessary detail or decoration.

Eng's production line continues to develop, mainly in two distinct areas: twisting wire forms and colorful geometric shapes. The Twist series is composed of wire-formed, tapered spirals, and the Whimsy series features colorful, asymmetrical shapes. Striking color enlivens both of these collections.

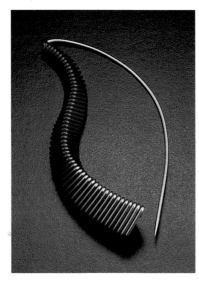

PIN   *Twist*
Aluminum and nickel
Fabricated, anodized,
and dyed

63

BRACELET   *Whimsy*
Aluminum
Textured, anodized, and dyed

When I have an idea or a flash of inspiration, I'll do a simple sketch, sometimes just a scribble. Next, I complete a quick mock-up in metal. If the design still seems promising, a prototype follows. After adjustments and fine-tuning, I determine the most time- and cost-effective way of producing the various components.

I use several methods, including die-stamping and jigs, and I cut out shapes with equipment such as band saws, milling machines, sheet metal shears, and lasers. My studio is equipped to handle most of these operations, but I job out processes such as laser cutting. I do not use any type of casting, because it is incompatible with the anodizing process. Once the shapes are cut, I apply surface textures by hand, drill holes, and remove burrs

technique

PIN *Whimsy Box*
Aluminum
Printed, textured,
fabricated, anodized,
and dyed

and rough edges with finishing wheels, abrasive papers,

or files. I create the wire structure of the Twist series by

wrapping aluminum wire around a jig or shaped-steel

mandrel that I make

myself. Then the

pieces are ready

to be anodized. Each piece

is pressure-fit or tension-fit on a titanium or

aluminum rack, then chemically cleaned, and, finally,

suspended in an anodizing bath. Then each rack is vat-dyed

to the desired color and chemically sealed. The racks are

hung to air-dry. Later, I assemble these colorful elements

into finished pieces of jewelry.

65

ENG

PIN *Whimsy Box*
Aluminum
Textured, patterned,
fabricated, anodized,
and dyed

EARRINGS *Whimsy*
Aluminum
Textured, anodized, and dyed

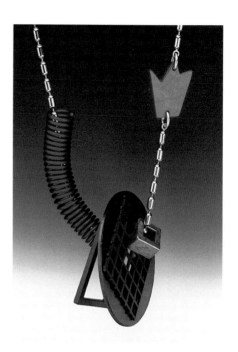

NECKPIECE *Multiple Floaters*
Aluminum and bar chain
Textured, fabricated, anodized, and dyed

Bracelets *Twist Bangle*
Aluminum
Fabricated, anodized, and dyed

PIN *Sawtooth*
Aluminum
Textured, fabricated,
anodized, and dyed

COLLAR *Shimmer*
Aluminum and hematite
Fabricated, anodized, and dyed

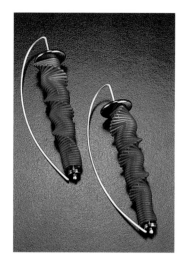

EARRINGS
Squiggle Twist
Aluminum, sterling silver,
and hematite
Fabricated, anodized,
and dyed

67

peggy eng

NECKPIECES
Twist
Aluminum, hematite,
and black onyx
Fabricated, anodized,
and dyed

EARRINGS
Nautilus
Aluminum and niobium
Fabricated, anodized,
and dyed

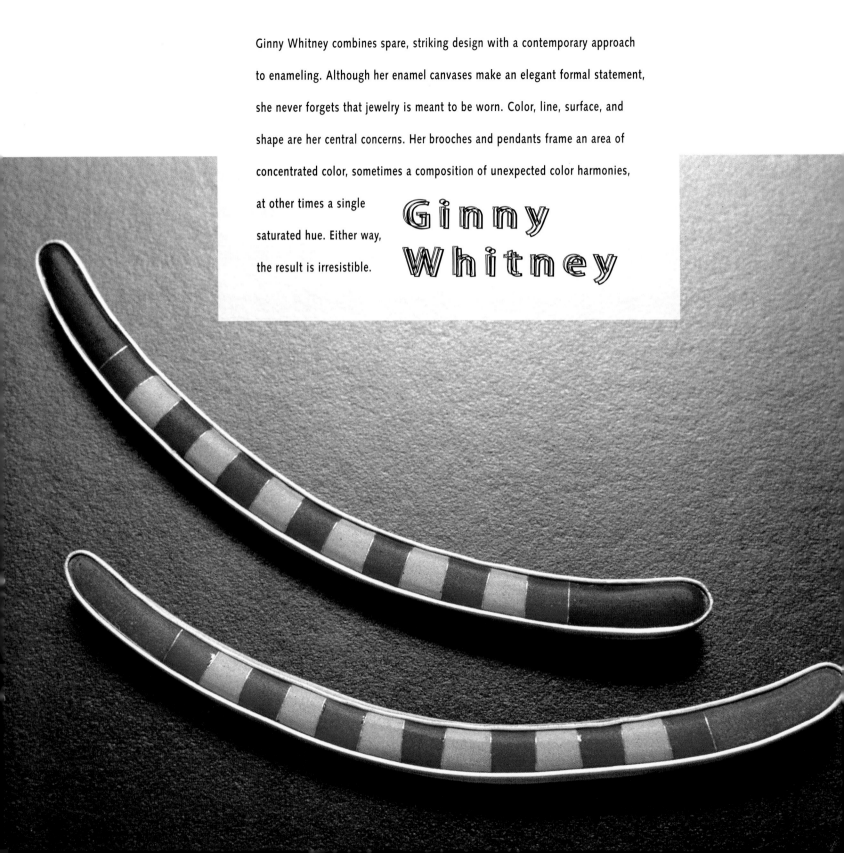

Ginny Whitney combines spare, striking design with a contemporary approach to enameling. Although her enamel canvases make an elegant formal statement, she never forgets that jewelry is meant to be worn. Color, line, surface, and shape are her central concerns. Her brooches and pendants frame an area of concentrated color, sometimes a composition of unexpected color harmonies, at other times a single saturated hue. Either way, the result is irresistible.

Ginny Whitney

These bold compositions are inspired by Whitney's mature artistry. She understands that color has movement, direction, and visual weight, moving forward or receding in relation to other colors. Line also forms an important visual element in her cloisonné jewelry. The individual cloisons contain and outline separate areas of color. In the past, Whitney worked with the ubiquitous fine silver cloisonné wire. Now, to achieve her signature black line, she works with the unorthodox choice of iron. Equally important is the line on which the pendant hangs—at first Whitney used a black neoprene cord, but more recently she has switched to sterling silver cable. It must create just the right curve in graceful relation to the pendant.

Inspired by a description of Chinese enamels, Whitney has revived their distinctive "eggshell" finish. Although laborious to achieve, the beautiful matte surface complements her opaque palette of intense colors.

Whitney's first collection consisted of brooches. She naturally gravitated to long, narrow shapes, some curved like a smile and others straight. She liked the play of the brooch's angle, from vertical to horizontal, when worn on the lapel. The transition to pendants came when Whitney herself wanted to wear them on a cable. The individual monochromatic shapes of the pendants seem like the individual components of a piece of cloisonné, now speaking on their own.

PENDANT
Fine silver, sterling silver, and enamel
Enameled and constructed

BROOCHES
Fine silver, sterling silver, and cloisonné enamel
Enameled and constructed

69

I like making jewelry that is simple, visually strong, and beautiful. Behind a seemingly simple piece lie much thought, preparation, and hard work. The strongest draw to working with enamel is the color—mixing three or four colors together can result in some very subtle effects.

My pieces often begin with a joyous, light-hearted image. The design may be a vision of the finished piece, complete in color, balance, and scale. Or it may be a black and white sketch of the wire work, or merely an outline.

technique

Even as I start to work, I can visualize the end result. I think of how it's going to be worn on a moving body. The color, whether strong or subtle, should enhance the fabric it will be worn on. I always consider what clothing does for jewelry and what jewelry does for clothing.

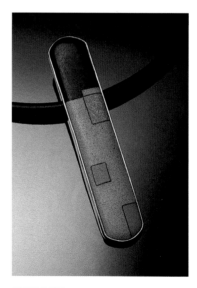

PENDANT
Fine silver, sterling silver, cloisonné enamel, and neoprene
Enameled and constructed

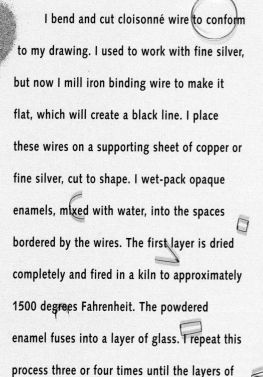

I bend and cut cloisonné wire to conform to my drawing. I used to work with fine silver, but now I mill iron binding wire to make it flat, which will create a black line. I place these wires on a supporting sheet of copper or fine silver, cut to shape. I wet-pack opaque enamels, mixed with water, into the spaces bordered by the wires. The first layer is dried completely and fired in a kiln to approximately 1500 degrees Fahrenheit. The powdered enamel fuses into a layer of glass. I repeat this process three or four times until the layers of

fused enamel reach the height of the wire. Then I hand-stone the piece with a carborundum stick and water until it is smooth and matte.

By filing, sawing, and soldering, I construct a setting from gold or silver that will present and protect the enamel. The matte metal surface complements the surface of the enamel. When completed, a successful piece always returns that original sense of joy and humor.

71

WHITNEY

BROOCH
24-karat gold, fine silver, sterling silver,
and cloisonné enamel
Enameled and constructed

BROOCH
24-karat gold, sterling silver, and cloisonné enamel
Enameled and constructed

BROOCH
24-karat gold, fine silver,
sterling silver, and cloisonné enamel
Enameled and constructed

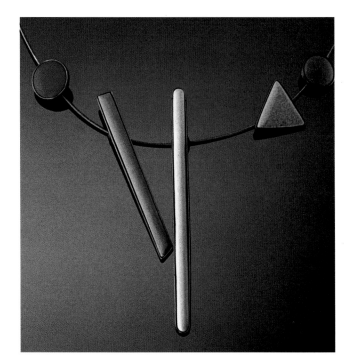

NECKPIECE
Fine silver, sterling silver, and enamel
Enameled and constructed

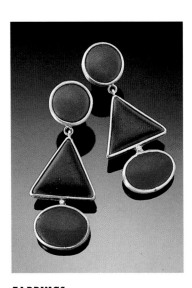

EARRINGS
24-karat gold, fine silver, sterling
silver, and cloisonné enamel
Enameled and constructed

PENDANT
24-karat gold, sterling silver,
and cloisonné enamel
Enameled and constructed

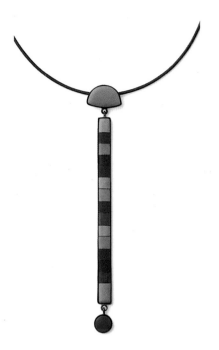

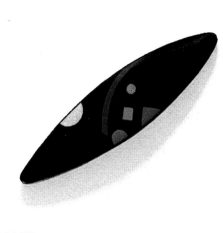

BROOCH
Fine silver, sterling silver,
and cloisonné enamel
Enameled and constructed

PENDANT
Fine silver, sterling silver, iron,
and cloisonné enamel
Enameled and constructed

NECKPIECE
Fine silver, sterling silver, iron,
and cloisonné enamel
Enameled and constructed

ginny whitney

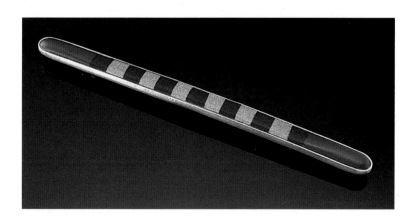

BROOCH
Fine silver, sterling silver, iron, 24-karat gold, and cloisonné enamel
Enameled and constructed

PENDANT
Fine silver, sterling silver,
iron, and cloisonné enamel
Enameled and constructed

In Mary Kanda's mosaic jewelry, purity of color glows in simplicity of form. Her innovative mosaic technique cunningly combines color, texture, and pattern framed by

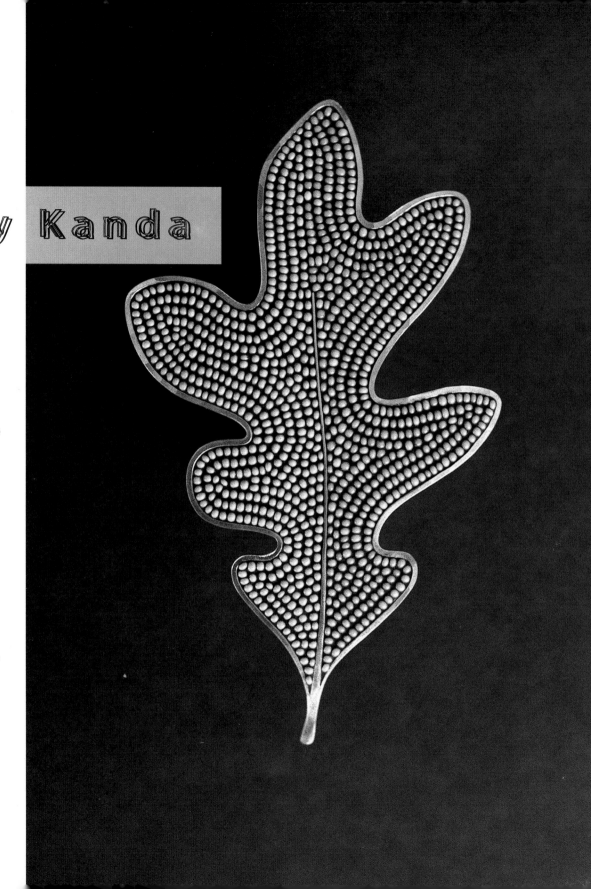

Mary Kanda

organic shapes of silver. Her signature jewelry represents a lifetime creative journey. From her father, she learned woodworking skills; she studied ceramics at the San Francisco Art Institute. A custom glass-etching studio was Kanda's foray into the world of art and commerce.

In the mid-1970s, she moved to Santa Fe, New Mexico. Sharing her studio with a jeweler, she became fascinated by the jeweler's tools and processes. She taught herself to enamel, which became the basis of her first production jewelry line. But she had no training as a jeweler. Kanda's strategy was to work in a local production house and learn her skills on the job from the cowboy metalsmiths. Still wanting more formal instruction, she cofounded the New Mexico Metalsmiths Association in 1988 to initiate a series of visiting artists workshops.

It was the artistic world beyond the jeweler's bench, however, that impressed and nourished Kanda. Santa Fe's galleries, museums, and Indian and ethnographic markets inspired her with their Navajo blankets and jewelry, Inuit ivory, African masks and ironwork, Kuba cloth, Tibetan prayer beads, Plains Indian bead and quillwork, Hopi baskets, and Mimbres pottery. The color sensibilities and shapes of twentieth-century painting, in the work of the Fauves, Arthur Dove, and Milton Avery, also influenced Kanda.

If New Mexico was the crucible, then her move to New England in 1991 has been the catalyst for Kanda to test and refine her work. Her jewelry, which brings together bright silver, colorful seed beads, and matte cement, speaks simply and directly. She combines color in unexpected ways and with a control of contrasting materials. Each piece vibrates with quiet energy.

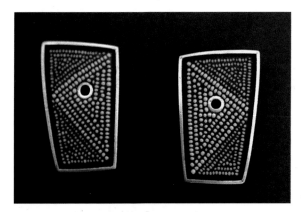

EARRINGS *Rectangle*
Sterling silver, glass beads, and portland cement
Fabricated and inlaid mosaic

PIN *Yellow Oak*
Sterling silver, glass beads, and portland cement
Fabricated and inlaid mosaic

I try to make sketches of ideas as they come up—enough to take note of the idea—and then develop them more fully later. In my work, metal defines each shape, and shapes refer to the natural world—the leaves that I

technique

have collected or my harvest of summer garden vegetables. The fabricated silver is first embossed with a soft, woven texture, and then finished with a raised, hammered bezel edge, which will contain the active color field. The opaque seed beads are my palette, contributing color, texture, line, and pattern relationships. Using tweezers and a magnifying glass, I meticulously place the beads in a pattern that reiterates and reinforces the silver silhouette. Mortar permanently secures the mosaic of beads.

76

PIN
Summer Vegetable series: Tomato
**Sterling silver, glass beads,
and portland cement
Fabricated and inlaid mosaic**

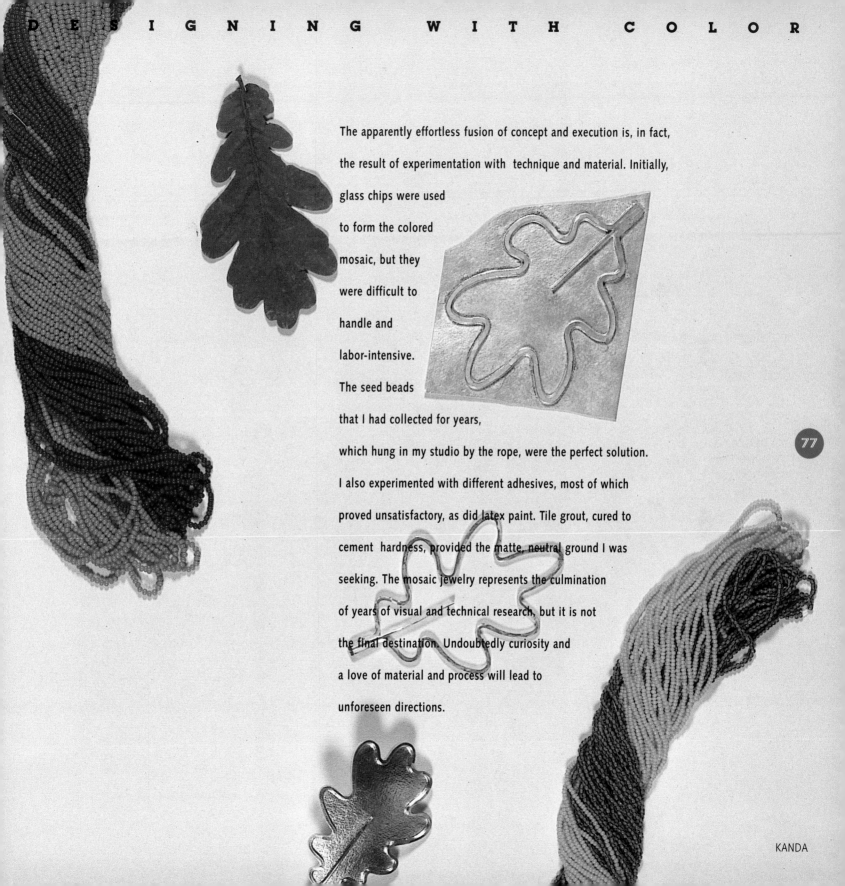

The apparently effortless fusion of concept and execution is, in fact,

the result of experimentation with technique and material. Initially,

glass chips were used

to form the colored

mosaic, but they

were difficult to

handle and

labor-intensive.

The seed beads

that I had collected for years,

which hung in my studio by the rope, were the perfect solution.

I also experimented with different adhesives, most of which

proved unsatisfactory, as did latex paint. Tile grout, cured to

cement hardness, provided the matte, neutral ground I was

seeking. The mosaic jewelry represents the culmination

of years of visual and technical research, but it is not

the final destination. Undoubtedly curiosity and

a love of material and process will lead to

unforeseen directions.

77

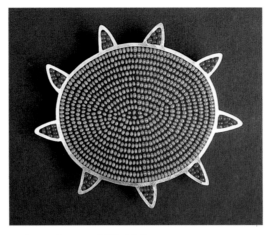

PIN   *Day and Night Sun*
Sterling silver, glass beads, and portland cement
Fabricated and inlaid mosaic

PIN   *Tulip Poplar Leaf*
Sterling silver, glass beads,
and portland cement
Fabricated and inlaid mosaic

mary kanda

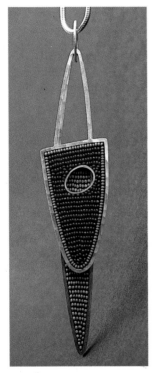

78

PENDANT   *Sub*
Sterling silver, glass beads,
and portland cement
Fabricated and inlaid mosaic

PIN   *Harlequin Leaf*
Sterling silver, glass beads, and portland cement
Fabricated and inlaid mosaic

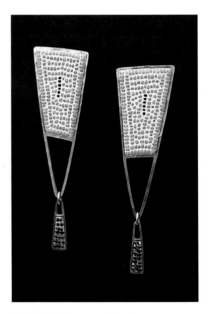

EARRINGS   *Drop*
Sterling silver, glass beads,
and portland cement
Fabricated and inlaid mosaic

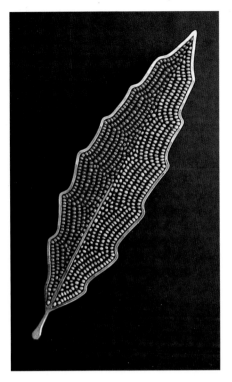

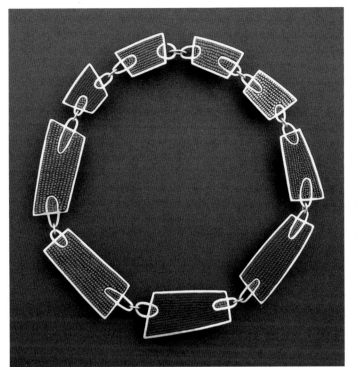

NECKLACE
Blue
Sterling silver,
glass beads, and
portland cement
Fabricated and
inlaid mosaic

PIN *Yellow Chestnut Oak Leaf*
Sterling silver, glass beads,
and portland cement
Fabricated and inlaid mosaic

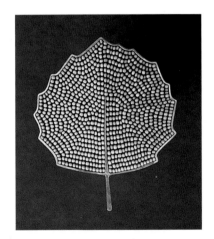

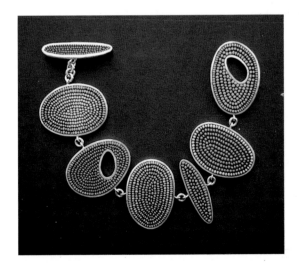

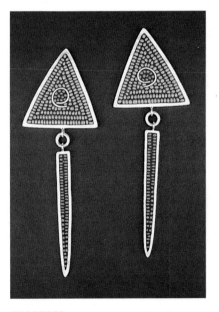

PIN *Toothed Poplar Leaf*
Sterling silver, glass beads,
and portland cement
Fabricated and inlaid mosaic

BRACELET *Link*
Sterling silver, glass beads, and portland cement
Fabricated and inlaid mosaic

EARRINGS
Triangle with Spiral and Drops
Sterling silver, glass beads, and
portland cement
Fabricated and inlaid mosaic

With a painter's love of color, David Urso has introduced paint pigment, graphics, herbs and spices, and color photocopies into his signature jewelry. His first pieces to combine metal structure with colored epoxy resin were the Mangled bracelets. The saturated colors were created by layering pigment mixed with epoxy, gradually building from opaque, to translucent, to transparent. He then carved into the hardened resin to create a striking juxtaposition of bright urban color and neo-primitive form.

David Urso

Fishing lures and Eskimo tools inspired the Pod series. Urso constructed the dimensional, organic forms out of aluminum and silver, which formed the canvases for his vibrant painting. Their color sensibilities and patterns reveal the influence of pop art, body tattoos, and contemporary graphics.

Urso responded to the economic recession of the early 1990s by constructing his metal housings from brass and bronze and limiting his palette to red, white, and black pigment. At the health food store, Urso thought of experimenting with herbs and spices in his jewelry. Rosemary, lavender, poppy seeds, paprika, dill, and sassafras were mixed with the epoxy resin to add color and texture—and sometimes even aroma! The reaction to this new work was immediate and enthusiastic.

Innovation continues to characterize Urso's work—as does a desire to incorporate contemporary materials. Most recently, he has embedded color photocopies in clear epoxy

resin, in the Charm necklaces and the Cameo bracelets. The delicate patterns and images are enigmatic, resembling antique mosaics or cameos. These modern hieroglyphs (he especially favors hearts, crosses, and spirals) invite personal interpretation and universal connection.

81

BELT   *Tiny Square Symbol*
Sterling silver, paint pigments,
color photocopies, and epoxy resin
Cast and inlaid epoxy

PIN   *Shield*
Bronze, paint pigments, poppy seeds, and epoxy resin
Fabricated and inlaid epoxy

Using metal as a form and canvas, I have learned to work with resins and paint pigments in combination with natural herbs and fibers, embedding them into clear epoxy resin to "lock them in time." In my recent work, I have created necklaces and bracelets by linking

technique

slightly misshapen domed circles and pillowed squares. They must have just the right crookedness—I don't want hard edges to frame their organic shapes.

My signature work is a contemporary production line of earrings, bracelets, rings, pins, and necklaces. As a production jeweler, I have to produce quantity. I fabricate the prototype from wire and sheet metal, simply working with an idea of what I want to do. For example, if I am thinking of a symbol such as a cross, I may make a dozen until I get the right one.

82

PINS *Starfish*
Bronze, paint pigments, sassafras,
and epoxy resin
Fabricated and inlaid epoxy

From this original model, I cast multiples in

bronze or sterling silver. The casting houses the epoxy

resin, which is embedded with color pigments, herbs,

or virtually anything to achieve the desired color and

texture. Color is always the most important part of any

piece. The pleasure of exploring color combinations

makes each collection new. After the piece has been

83

inlaid with tinted resin and cured to hardness, I grind it

with a stone wheel to reveal the underlying

symbol or pattern. Then I scrub, polish, and lacquer it.

Finally, I connect it with a jump

ring to other pieces to form

earrings, bracelets, or necklaces.

URSO

PIN *Mangled Spiral*
Sterling silver, paint pigment, and epoxy resin
Fabricated

RINGS *Venetian and Cross*
Bronze, paint pigments, kelp, sand,
chile powder, and epoxy resin
Cast, fabricated, and inlaid epoxy

84

BRACELETS *Mangled*
Sterling silver, paint pigment, and epoxy resin
Fabricated and inlaid epoxy

BRACELETS *Symbol*
Brass, paint pigments, herbs, and epoxy resin
Cast, epoxy, and inlaid epoxy

PINS *Pod*
Aluminum, nickel silver,
paint pigments, and epoxy resin
Fabricated and inlaid epoxy

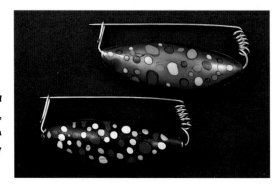

NECKLACE   *Tiny Symbol*
Sterling silver, paint pigments,
herbs, and epoxy resin
Cast and inlaid epoxy

BRACELETS   *Cameo*
Sterling silver, paint pigments, color photocopy, and epoxy resin
Cast and inlaid epoxy

david urso

EARRINGS   *Target*
Sterling silver, paint
pigments, and epoxy resin
Fabricated

85

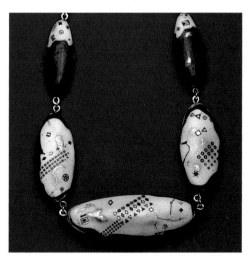

NECKLACE   *Pod*
Sterling silver, gold leaf, nickel silver,
graphics, paint pigments, and epoxy resin
Fabricated

PENDANTS   *Pole*
Sterling silver, paint
pigments, and epoxy resin
Fabricated

designing with alternative materials

Often when a jeweler chooses to work with unconventional materials—such as handmade paper, found objects, rubber, or graphite—he or she establishes a new idiom, inventing new structures for jewelry. Jocelyn Chateauvert, who designs jewelry based on her translucent abaca paper, and Thomas Mann, who creates a culture of techno-romantic jewelry, are just such jewelers.

Working with enamel, graphite, and mica, Joan Parcher's jewelry displays an economy of form inseparable from sensuous material. She tweaks our reverence for

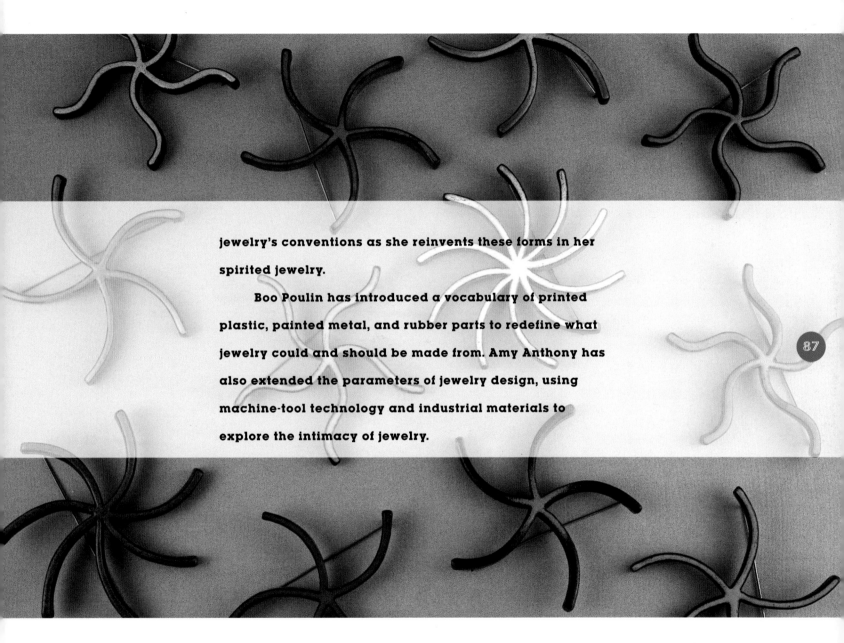

jewelry's conventions as she reinvents these forms in her spirited jewelry.

Boo Poulin has introduced a vocabulary of printed plastic, painted metal, and rubber parts to redefine what jewelry could and should be made from. Amy Anthony has also extended the parameters of jewelry design, using machine-tool technology and industrial materials to explore the intimacy of jewelry.

87

JOAN PARCHER
BROOCHES
Copper and enamel
Electroformed, enameled, and patinated

Laughter—effervescent, spontaneous, intelligent laughter—characterizes Jocelyn

Jocelyn Chateauvert

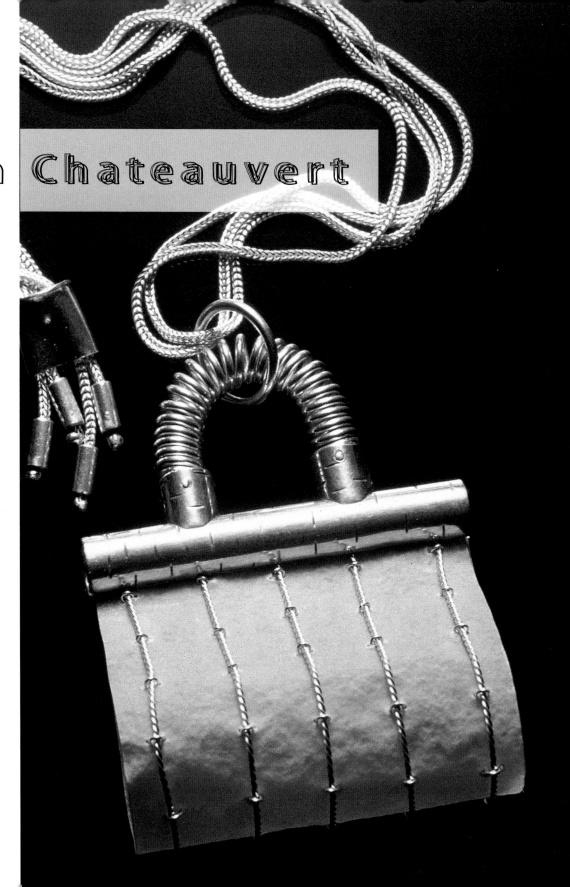

Chateauvert and her handmade paper jewelry collection. Most of her work is connected to a story with an element of humor. She celebrates paper's structure and translucency, complementing it with silver's opacity and solidity. The combination presents a yin-and-yang—the paper made from fiber and water, the metal forged from earth and fire. Her work challenges conventional definitions of jewelry.

Raised on the arts, Chateauvert was enrolled in classes at the Des Moines Art Center starting at age four. At the University of Iowa, she studied jewelry and metalsmithing, and also began her romance with handmade paper. She loved the physical paper-making process and the aesthetic qualities of paper, combining it with silver to create sculptural forms.

Her artist's residency at London's Middlesex Polytechnic affirmed her commitment to challenge the parameters of what jewelry could be. She spent four years refining the unlikely combination of paper and metal in jewelry.

Her work is sensuous on many levels. The tactile material invites touch. The structure of both the paper itself and its relationship to the metal is technically interesting and can also be richly evocative. For example, in "Eve, Clothes Optional," a layered fig leaf on a long supple chain, Chateauvert suggests an imagined narrative, the erotic sensation of paper against skin, and the private ritual of adornment.

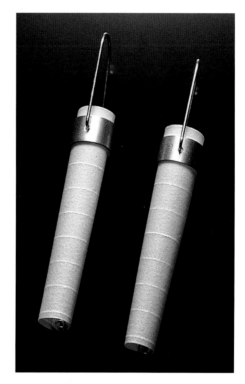

EARRINGS *Cylinders*
Sterling and handmade paper
Fabricated

PENDANT *Weekender*
Sterling silver, fine silver, and handmade paper
Fabricated

90

I usually start with drawings, but these are mere thumbnail sketches and only suggest a direction. From there my best success comes from directly working with paper and then looking for complementary metalwork. Of course, on occasion I get a total vision of a piece.

I work with abaca paper, a variation of a traditional paper made in the Philippines. It is archival, flexible, and naturally resistant to water. Although light in weight, it has solidity

technique and presence. I make the paper in my studio, working with a Hollander beater, molds, a hydraulic press, and felts. I use an awl both to mark the silhouette for cutting and to define an edge by compressing the fibers. In other pieces, I prefer to leave a deckle edge. My concern in

EARRINGS   *Niagara Falls*
Sterling silver and handmade paper
Fabricated

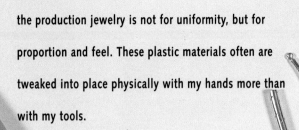

the production jewelry is not for uniformity, but for proportion and feel. These plastic materials often are tweaked into place physically with my hands more than with my tools.

After developing the paper elements and their relationship to the body, I then house them in the simplest possible metal lines. I fabricate the silver housing, often incorporating embossed or hammered surfaces. I enjoy hand-sawing and use the technique to graze slits in silver tubing or to make cutouts.

Paper is primary. It inspires me. Although I feel that I am still developing vocabulary for the work, my direction is clear. In moving from architectural to more complex organic constructed forms, with less metal housing, I invite more physical interaction between the object and the wearer. In the most interesting work, the paper has formal and structural autonomy.

jocelyn chateauvert

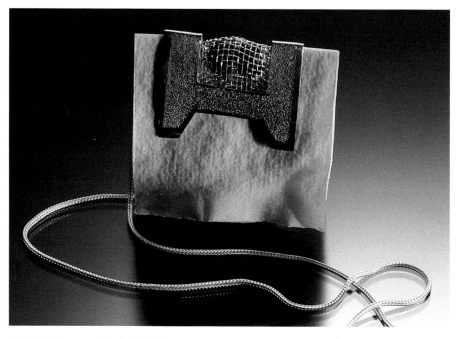

PENDANT *Rice and Beans*
Sterling silver, fine silver mesh, handmade paper, and beans
Embossed and fabricated

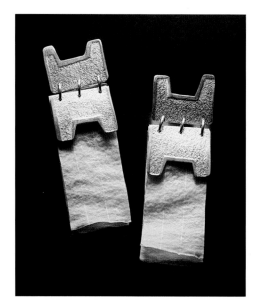

EARRINGS *RBE*
Sterling silver and handmade paper
Embossed and fabricated

PENDANT *Volume 1*
Sterling silver and handmade paper
Fabricated

EARRINGS *Leaf Forms*
Sterling silver and handmade paper
Fabricated

EARRINGS   *Twin Peaks*
Sterling silver and handmade paper
Fabricated

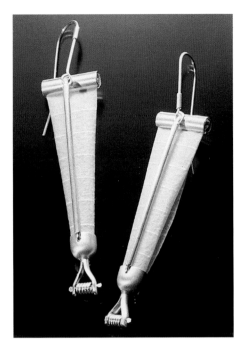

EARRINGS   *Speedy Vacs*
Sterling silver and handmade paper
Fabricated

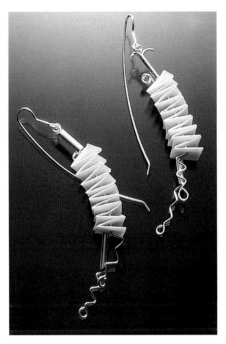

EARRINGS   *Jacks*
Sterling silver and handmade paper
Fabricated

93

PENDANT
Sterling silver and handmade paper
Fabricated

EARRINGS   *Handbags*
Sterling silver and handmade paper
Fabricated

PENDANT   *Eve, Clothes Optional*
Sterling silver and handmade paper
Fabricated

Boo Poulin

Boo Poulin's work is characterized by precise craftsmanship, spare forms, and richly articulated surfaces.

In the early 1980s, Poulin began her career by making a series of stainless steel pins with graphic tape incorporated on the surfaces. This unusual combination sparked an ongoing desire to redefine jewelry in terms of what it could and should be made of. She later developed custom colors and print patterns on

plastic, and she created jewelry that incorporated printed plastic, painted metal, and rubber.

Although Poulin's finished pieces continue to be unconventional, her latest work marks a return to more traditional materials and techniques. Silver is cast, heavily textured, and oxidized; the silver forms are then combined with plastic or steel cable. These designs exhibit the same juxtaposition of extremes that has characterized her jewelry from the start. Poulin elevates the most basic of materials through the strength and simplicity of her design.

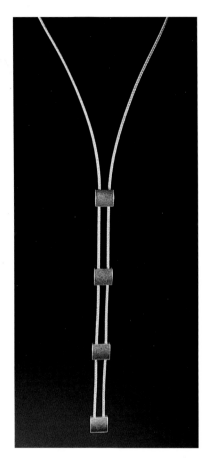

NECKLACE
Sterling silver and steel cable
Cast and fabricated

BRACELET
Sterling silver
Cast and fabricated

The design process for me is a progression of ideas that ultimately creates a unique visual language. Sometimes I will make very quick drawings that are often accompanied by words. Simultaneously, I collect materials that I find suggestive: rusted metal parts, hardware store paraphernalia, or even machine pieces, such as gears—in other words, whatever I might find that attracts me visually.

technique

In the past, I worked with small industrial shops that produced parts to my specifications; then I finished the jewelry in my studio. The finishing often included sanding, hand-coloring plastic, texturing metals, and some assembly. I used rubber O-rings as connectors, and I incorporated screws both for their visual interest and as a means of joining the alternative materials (plastic, aluminum, rubber) that I was fond of using at the time.

PIN
Sterling silver, plastic, and rubber
Die-cut and fabricated

Since I have returned to silver in my work, my technical concerns have changed. Casting is now my primary means of achieving an inventory of shapes. I make prototypes that are either fabricated in metal or carved in wax. I work out all technical concerns at this stage: mechanical considerations are incorporated, weight is factored in, and proportions are determined. Even though my primary material is currently silver, my obsession with color and surface remains. In order to finish my pieces, I file them heavily to create an interesting surface, and I oxidize them to change the color of the silver to a rich gray. Although nothing is highly polished, everything shines.

97

POULIN

BRACELET
Sterling silver
Cast and fabricated

NECKLACE
Sterling silver
Cast and fabricated

NECKLACE
Sterling silver
Cast and fabricated

BRACELETS
Sterling silver and steel
Cast and fabricated

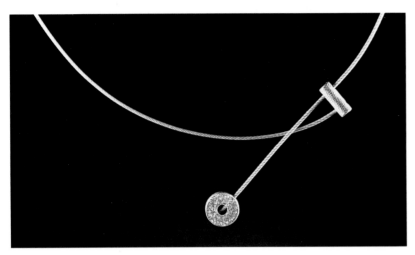

NECKLACE
Sterling silver and steel cable

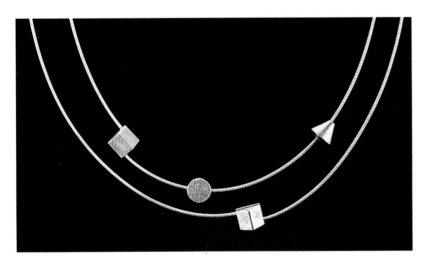

TWO NECKLACES
Sterling silver and steel cable
Cast and fabricated

EARRINGS
Sterling silver
Cast and
fabricated

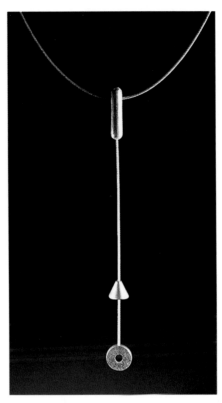

NECKLACE
Sterling silver and steel cable
Cast and fabricated

boo poulin

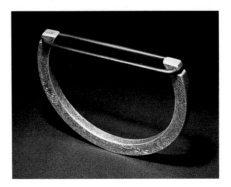

BRACELET
Sterling silver and rubber
Cast and fabricated

During the late 1970s and early 1980s, Thomas Mann experimented with collage and assemblage, applying these quintessentially twentieth-century techniques to the creation of jewelry. Out of these investigations he formulated a vocabulary of material, technique, and design that he calls "techno-romantic," defined by romantic imagery made of nostalgic and high-tech materials, from tintype photographs to printed circuit boards. His collage technique allows Mann to layer several ideas and concepts into a small physical space. The found object, cornerstone and catalyst for each design, speaks of the serendipitous encounter.

Thomas Mann

During the formative years of the techno-romantic style, the "look" focused on found objects—salvage from the space and electronics industries, machine parts, and plastics. As the audience for the work grew, it became more difficult to find enough of this material. In the mid-1980s, Mann started to make parts that *appear* to be found objects.

Techno-romanticism is more than an aesthetic. It forms a language to express Mann's strongly held political and social views—he hopes to transform our relationship to technology, recognizing both our connection to and alienation from it. He wants his work to be evaluated on the basis of image and message content rather than the value of materials; thus he deliberately chooses to work with nonprecious metals—brass, bronze, stainless steel, copper, aluminum. (Sterling silver is the only exception.) Going beyond the usual expectations of adornment, his amulets express wearable ideas. His intent to provide as much aesthetic content as possible at an accessible price has contributed to the enormous success of his work.

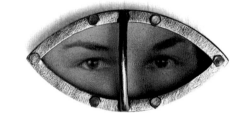

PINS *Caged Eye Photo*
Silver, brass, acrylic,
and photograph; Fabricated

PIN *Hand*
Bronze, brass, and laminated Lucite
Fabricated

101

technique   I feel that I participate, in a metaphysical manner, in the delivery of meaning and definition to the tribe. I make little mechanisms for people to use to construct their own realities. I draw almost everything I make. Drawing is the stage at which the idea and the intention cross over from the possible to the probable. I start with design investigations for the one-of-a-kind pieces, and find within them the elements that will feed the production line. In the process of working at the bench,

I make design decisions about the prototype that will affect the look of the piece and the method of production. Often I discover a little fabrication trick.

The very nature of collage determines that cold connections form the primary fabrication technique. I use rivets, stitching, slots and tabs, and nuts and bolts to join the different

PIN   *Collage Running House*
Brass, bronze, and laminated Lucite
Fabricated

elements and layers. Along with traditional metalsmithing techniques, I use die-forming, photo-etching, and sandblasting. My attitude toward material, technique, and concept defines the techno-romantic idiom. I work with a variety of materials from different sources, in which each element contributes to an integrated narrative and formal structure. A flat, chased graphic background of brass, bronze, nickel, or silver is built up with collage elements of various materials. With miniature bolts, I attach laminated two-color acrylic slabs, cut as diagonal striping. Perforated screening of various sizes and materials serves as the matrix for attaching collage objects. These elements work together to produce a dense surface of ornamentation with movement and color. Hearts are a recurring image and theme in my work, as is containment. Small spaces are often filled with entrapped or encapsulated objects.

The work is labor-intensive. It is simply not possible to make everything by hand. Using tools and machinery to make the process cost-effective is simply common sense. But it's important to me that the work maintains a high level of technical quality and retains the spirit of the handmade process.

103

MANN

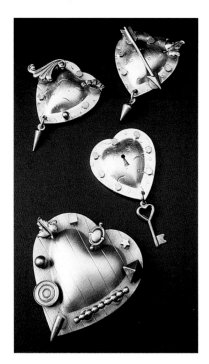

PIN *Fertility Goddess*
Silver, bronze, brass, laminated
Lucite, iron, and Micarta
Fabricated

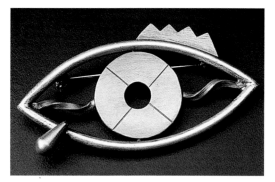

PIN *Eye*
Silver, brass, and nickel
Fabricated

thomas mann

BRACELETS *Locomotion*
Bronze
Constructed and fabricated

PINS *Collage Chamber Heart*
Silver, brass, bronze, and nickel
Die-formed and fabricated

EARRINGS *Collage Hand*
Nickel, brass, glass, and Lucite
Fabricated

MONEY CLIPS *Abstract*
Nickel and bronze
Fabricated

PIN
Collage Torso
Silver, bronze,
aluminum, and
stainless steel
Fabricated

NECKLACE   *Three-D Heart*
Silver, brass, bronze, and copper
Die-formed and fabricated

NECKLACE
Abstract Charm
Silver, brass,
bronze, and nickel
Fabricated

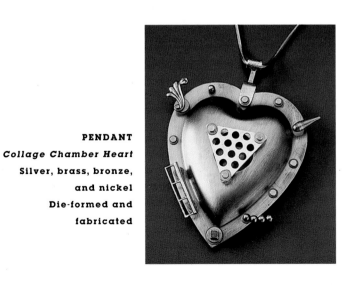

PENDANT
Collage Chamber Heart
Silver, brass, bronze,
and nickel
Die-formed and
fabricated

Joan Parcher's earliest childhood memories are of designing and figuring out ways to make jewelry. At four years of age, she discovered wire-cutting pliers. Later, she collected discarded "junk" and, with a hammer and determination, formed it into rings and necklaces.

To this enduring passion for jewelry, Parcher joins a love for materials; her favorites include graphite, mica, other stones, and enamel. Her jewelry designs are based on an understanding of their physical nature. She loves the process of enameling and the color of opaque enamels. Her Graphite Pendulum pendant, carved on the lathe, demonstrates Parcher's fascination with cause and effect. The graphite pendulum leaves a smudged shadow that records its movement across the wearer's body.

Joan Parcher

She contemplates designs and materials, sometimes for years, before incorporating them into her working vocabulary. The concept of two opposite things, a positive and a negative shape, on the end of a cable first occurred to her in the 1970s. It was another decade, however, before she finally made the Ball and Hoop Neckpiece. The incubation period for her recent mica jewelry was even longer.

Although she works equally well with both organic and geometric forms, the quintessential Parcher aesthetic is based upon simple, functional, well-designed, wearable objects. She fabricates the complex geometry of the Polyhedron and Hoop neckpiece from a simple four-sided pyramidal commercial finding. The simplicity and spontaneity of her Flower earrings transcend cliché: she domes a precut copper shape, dusts it with enamel powder,

adds a tumbled hematite bead, and then joins it to her own silver and gold earring finding. She reinvents the basic chain by using links of transparent mica. Parcher has wonderful fun giving pleasure through the jewelry she makes.

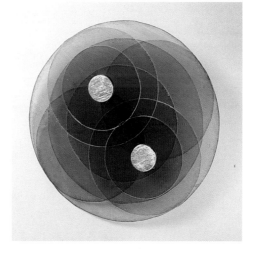

BROOCH   *Mica*
Sterling silver and mica
Pierced and fabricated

107

CHAIN   *Mica*
18-Karat gold and mica
Die-cut and fabricated

I like to learn about the nature of the materials that I work with. They inspire

me. I do lots of sketches and idea drawings, and I often have to

think about a piece for a long time before I actually make it. I use

simple shapes to allow the nature of the materials to predominate.

Graphite interests me because it makes a mark on almost everything

it touches. With mica, a lightweight, see-through stone, I can

make a thirteen-foot chain that is as light as a feather; or I can

layer it to make a transparent brooch.

The mica comes from India in sheets of varying thickness and colors,

from rose to slightly brown. I like to work with

the clearest available, which is silvery in tone.

technique

For the brooches, I lay out the design and score the surface with dividers—

or I use a template to mark the pattern of circles. Then I cut out the shape.

EARRINGS
Sterling silver and 24-karat vermeil
Cast and oxidized

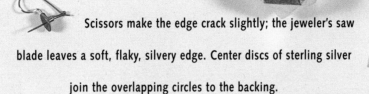

Scissors make the edge crack slightly; the jeweler's saw blade leaves a soft, flaky, silvery edge. Center discs of sterling silver join the overlapping circles to the backing.

I fabricate the chain from die-cut doughnut shapes of mica.

The process is identical to the most basic loop-in-loop wire chain: two closed rings are joined with an open link, which is then glued with epoxy. Multiplying this basic unit, I can make a chain of any length. The technique is deceptively simple. I have developed a feel for mica and a skill in handling it. I use the simplest possible closure—a link of thin sterling silver with an extension that is hammer-textured to harden the metal, then oxidized.

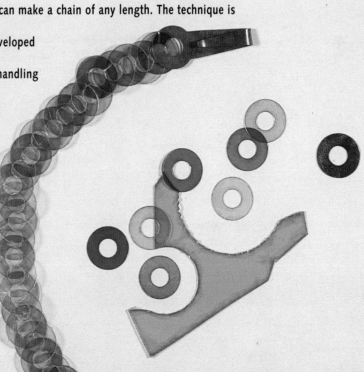

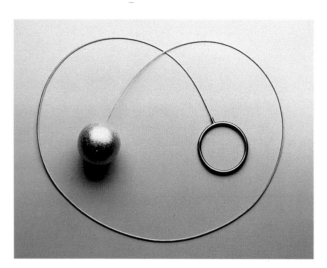

NECKPIECE   *Ball and Hoop*

24-karat gold leaf over sterling silver, and stainless steel

Fabricated and oxidized

BRACELETS

Copper and enamel

Electroformed, enameled, and patinated

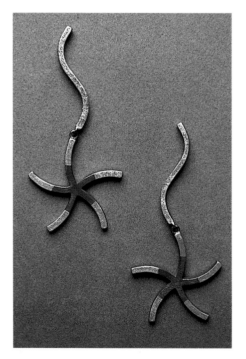

EARRINGS

Sterling silver and 24-karat vermeil

Cast and oxidized

PENDANT   [above and right]

Graphite Pendulum

Soft graphite, sterling silver, and stainless steel

Lathe-turned and fabricated

EARRINGS
Flower
Sterling silver, copper,
and enamel
Formed, enameled,
and oxidized

NECKLACES
Sterling silver
Cast

joan parcher

BRACELET
Polka Dot
Sterling silver and copper
Enameled and oxidized

NECKPIECE   *Polyhedron and Hoop*
23-karat gold leaf over sterling silver,
and stainless steel
Cast, fabricated, and oxidized

Machine-tool technology inspires Amy Anthony's precise, spare, yet playful brooches. Her machine aesthetic is fluently expressed in her materials—aluminum, steel, plastic—and in her design process, which she describes as series of decisions.

These decisions start with manipulation of the material. Anthony does not make drawings, but rather carves directly into the material with tool and die equipment, which includes horizontal and vertical mills, router, shaper,

Amy Anthony

and band saw. The machines introduce surface texture: grooves, scars, punches, scratches. Anthony then considers the direction of the piece. Often she will use traditional metalsmithing techniques to refine and complement the machined form. She may forge a surface to create a soft, broken, stressed edge, or she may file and sand the surface to remove the machine marks.

Imagery and content emerge from the process of making the piece: how one part is joined to another, how one part fits into another. Anthony describes her jewelry as drawings that exist in three dimensions; typically these "drawings" show a line in relation to a flat plane. She often presents a highly controlled, rigid relation between steel and aluminum, and then secures it with the most casual connection—a rubber band. Although the somber grays of stainless steel and aluminum reflect the subdued colors of the urban environment, Anthony introduces unexpected color by anodizing the aluminum.

When Anthony first set up her work-shop, she cut out all her parts with a hacksaw and then filed them square. As she has acquired more tools and equipment, she has changed her method of production. Now she uses the band saw to cut out parts, mills them square, and then hand-finishes each part. Although the level of precision was better when she completed each step by hand, new

tools and techniques have increased her aesthetic choices. Her next leap in machine technology will be the computer. CNC (computerized numerical control) equipment will enable her to reproduce prototypes more easily and efficiently.

113

BROOCH
Aluminum and stainless steel
Hand- and machine-fabricated

BROOCH
Aluminum, brass, and Delrin
Hand- and machine-fabricated

I tend to make changes and choices that allow me to reproduce production work with ease. For example, I chose plastic as a base material for my latest pieces. It is stable, lightweight, and neutral in color. It is also easy to manipulate and much easier to cut than aluminum and stainless steel.

The design process starts with a block of Delrin stock. I use the band saw and a coarse blade to cut down its thickness. I really like the texture of the rip cut, which provides inspiration for developing the rest of the piece. I cut two parallel edges. Then I use the shaper to cut two skinny triangles with angled walls—this gives the illusion of two planes, one smooth and one textured.

technique

Working on the lathe, I drill a hole in the center of some round aluminum stock. Then I ream the hole, to obtain accurate size and a smooth finish. On the milling machine, I cut two flat parallel surfaces—so the stock is no longer circular in cross-section. By using the hacksaw and cutting

114

BROOCH
Aluminum, stainless steel, and string
Hand- and machine-fabricated

the stock at an angle, I change the circle to an oval.

I then remove all saw marks by machine- and

hand-sanding. I make a second, angled cut to

separate the oval washer from the stock.

Before joining the aluminum to the plastic,

I machine down the thickness of the plastic. To make the

cold connections, I drill the aluminum with a tap drill.

Using the aluminum as a template, I transfer the center

of the holes onto the plastic and drill them out with

a clearance drill. From the back of the brooch, I counter-

sink two flat-headed screws into the plastic and then

thread them into the aluminum. I solder the brooch

finding onto a screwhead, drill and tap a hole in the

plastic, and finally screw it in.

ANTHONY

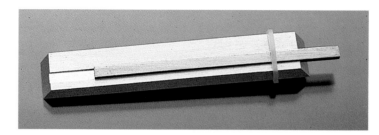

BROOCH
Aluminum, steel, and rubber band
Hand- and machine-fabricated

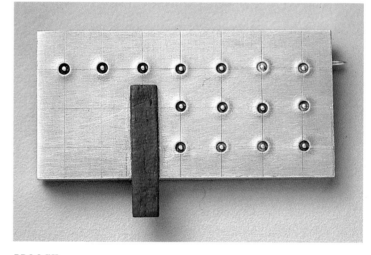

BROOCH
Aluminum and mahogany
Hand fabricated

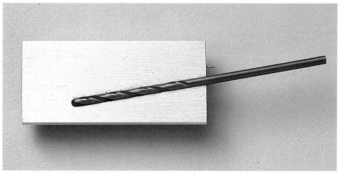

BROOCH
Aluminum and steel
Hand- and machine-fabricated

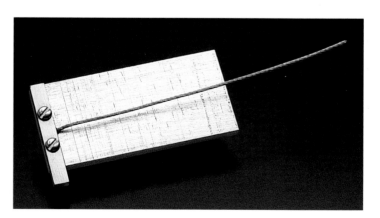

BROOCH
Aluminum, stainless steel, and steel
Hand- and machine-fabricated

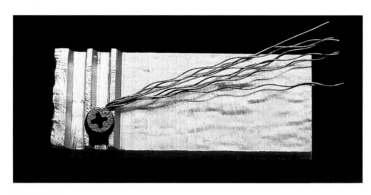

BROOCH
Aluminum and steel
Hand- and machine-fabricated

BROOCH
Aluminum, stainless steel, and ink
Hand- and machine-fabricated

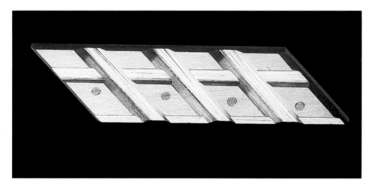

BROOCH
Aluminum and stainless steel
Hand- and machine-fabricated

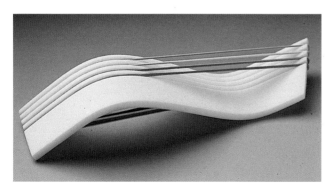

BRACELET
Teflon with colored rubber bands
Hand- and machine-fabricated

BROOCH
Stainless steel and Delrin
Hand- and machine-fabricated

Valerie Mitchell, Gabriella Kiss, and Catherine Butler use the human figure and other elements of the natural world for imagery and inspiration in their jewelry design.

Butler's animated figures are completely contemporary. In their attitudes and activities, they portray the humor and drama of everyday life.

designing from nature

Butler's direct approach to the process—creating form, texture, and color from flat sheet metal—gives her figures freshness and vitality.

Kiss studies the human figure, keenly observing hands and heads that she then precisely carves in wax.

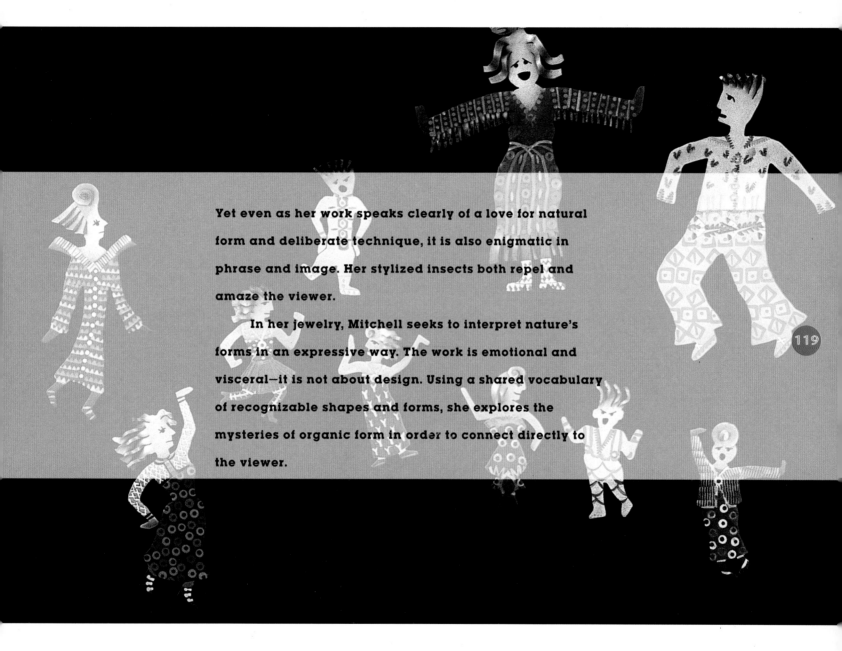

Yet even as her work speaks clearly of a love for natural form and deliberate technique, it is also enigmatic in phrase and image. Her stylized insects both repel and amaze the viewer.

In her jewelry, Mitchell seeks to interpret nature's forms in an expressive way. The work is emotional and visceral—it is not about design. Using a shared vocabulary of recognizable shapes and forms, she explores the mysteries of organic form in order to connect directly to the viewer.

119

CATHERINE BUTLER
PINS   *People*
Sterling silver, copper, and brass
Pierced, formed, stamped, oxidized,
and inlaid with colored epoxy

The search for structure defines the expressive jewelry of Valerie Mitchell. Her environment has always been the source for her imagery, from her first collection focusing on manmade structure and industrial materials, to her

Valerie Mitchell

gradual evolution toward organic form and the examination of patterns and shapes in nature.

In 1984, Mitchell's premier jewelry collection, which focused on industrial materials and products, enjoyed immediate recognition and success. She used a labor-intensive combination of cast, constructed, and electroformed parts. Mitchell pioneered techniques for electroformed jewelry, exploring its potential for dimensional form in order to create jewelry of volume with minimal mass.

Mitchell's Leaf collection, her most recent work, alludes to the simple pleasure of a walk in the woods. Close inspection hints that her amble would be anything but ordinary.

She says, "I like to look close and deep, past the surface and into the structure" of natural form. Mitchell is a naturalist whose works go beyond simple description of appearances. Her expressive forms are referential and interpretive. She looks at the specific—a leaf, a twig, a pod—to reveal both its abstract structure and the transcendent power of nature.

Although the soul of her work is its strong connection to nature, its emotional content lies in its appeal to the senses of sight and touch. It speaks of connectedness and experiential memory, of a longing for seasonal rhythms. Mitchell's jewelry refocuses a sated eye on the world of nature.

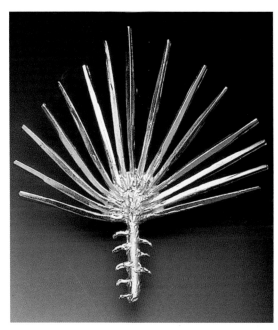

BROOCH   *Washington Palm*
Brass and gold plate

121

NECKLACES   *Eucalyptus series*
Sterling silver and vermeil
Cast and constructed

technique

I collect leaves, twigs, and plants (sometimes magnifying a section to study its structure), and then sketch directly from nature or from memory. My drawings, which are not about jewelry but about my personal imagery, inspire my one-of-a-kind jewelry. These, in turn, can lead to designs for the production jewelry. The one-offs are sculptural and abstract. The production jewelry is more referential and recognizable in its visual source. Together, they share an aesthetic and extend my working vocabulary.

I model in malleable wax, just concentrating on form. I use the wax to build dimensional form or skeletal structure, with a soft tactile surface. The modeled wax is the prototype from which a rubber mold is made. The mold is used to create wax multiples, which are then cast or electroformed.

BROOCHES *Leaf series*
Silver, brass, and gold plate
Cast and patinated

fifteen hours to build up a strong shell of copper over the wax. When the forming process is completed, I remove the elements from the bath and start to work the surfaces by

In the Pod necklace series, electroforming gives me the possibility of creating what I call "one-of-a-kind" multiples.

filing and polishing and possibly some patination. I boil and steam the core of wax out, leaving the hollow shell of copper. I continue filing, sanding, and polishing the forms. Then I can

From the rubber mold, I can reproduce the original form in wax multiples. With each of these individual wax elements, I file, texture, and rework the form. Then they are ready for the electroforming bath. It takes from six to

take the electroformed bead elements and incorporate them into a necklace.

Although I start with a wax form that has been reproduced, I can vary the way in which I finish the surface—how it is filed or sanded or polished—and how I color or patinate the copper—and how I configure the individual "beads." In this way, I can take an idea—a necklace inspired by the form of the honey mesquite pod—and rework it into a series of related pieces.

123

MITCHELL

EARRINGS *Fern*
Brass and gold plate
Cast

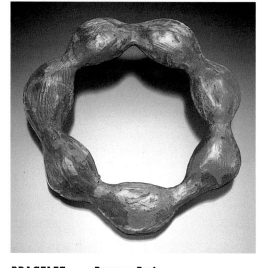

BRACELET *Pepper Pod*
Copper
Electroformed and patinated

BROOCH *Vortex*
Copper
Cast and patinated

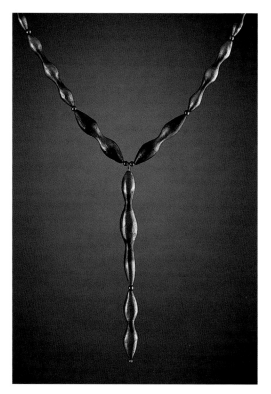

NECKLACE *Pod II*
Copper and 18-karat gold
Electroformed

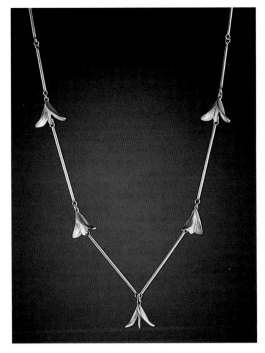

NECKLACE *Cedar Seed*
Sterling silver
Cast and constructed

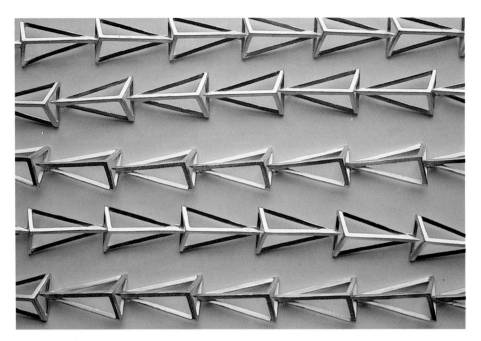

NECKLACES *Geo series*
Sterling silver and vermeil
Cast and constructed

BRACELETS *Cedar Seed, Structure, Pod, Rib Pod, Jade Leaf*
Brass, gold plate, copper
Cast, electroformed, and constructed

valerie mitchell

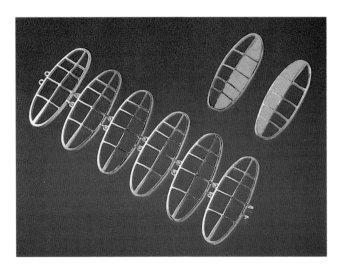

BRACELET AND EARRINGS *Cage*
Sterling silver and cement
Cast and constructed

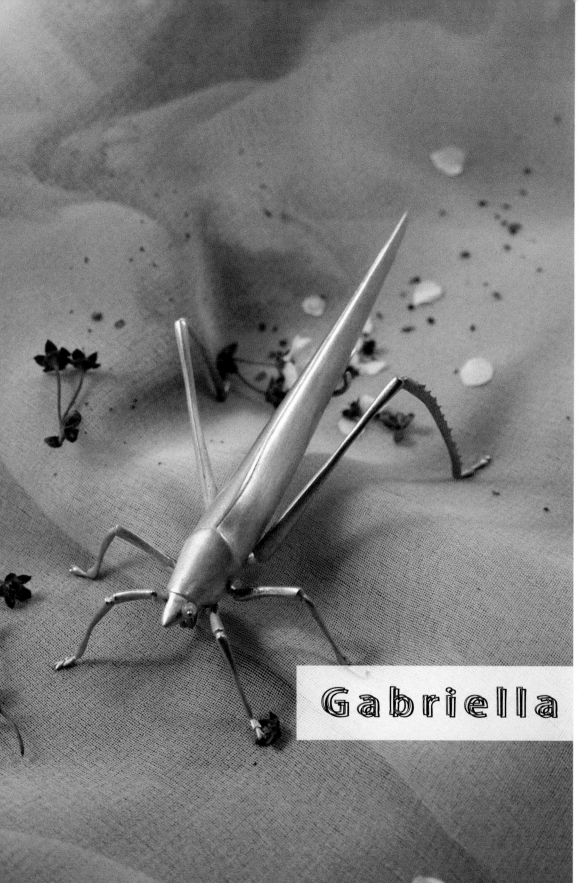

Gabriella Kiss

A gesturing hand, a blade of grass, an insect's wing—Gabriella Kiss uses these evocative details to suggest a larger narrative in her exquisite jewelry. Her sense of connection to family and friends, to the history of art, and to the natural world inspires the forms and images of her jewelry.

Even as an art student, Kiss carved her signature hand brooches. Each is a private homage to a revered artist: the sculptor Canova, the Italian mannerist Bronzino, the Austrian expressionist Schiele. In the Hand pin, the human hand, freed from a specific context, becomes a symbol to reveal character and life experience. Soft, feminine hands become a metaphor for a caring, tender touch. The bony angularity of Schiele's gesturing hands suggests an artistic personality working and creating.

Her detailed carvings of a nose, an ear, lips, a tearful eye ornament Kiss's inscribed ring bands. An engraved Latin inscription alludes to the visual image. They carry not only the artist's meaning, but also, in the language of gift giving, celebrate and commemorate attachment to family, friends, community.

The precision of Kiss's keenly observed insects, including praying mantises and grasshoppers, reveals an awe-inspiring beauty. The magnification of scale and the poised gesture give these stylized creatures a menacing presence—in spite of their elegant form and proportion. In her Blade of Grass with Leafhoppers cuff and her hair combs, Kiss situates her winged insects in particular landscapes. Because they exist in a separate space,

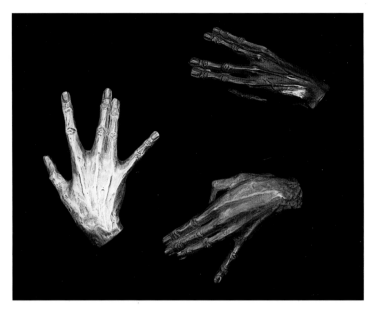

PINS *Schiele's Hands*
Sterling silver and bronze
Cast and oxidized

they seem less threatening. These dramatic hair combs recall those of the art nouveau jeweler René Lalique. The natural forms, the Japanese design sensibility, and the use of carved horn are part of his inspired legacy.

PIN *Grasshopper*
Sterling silver
Cast

The notion of doing something the best I can is the motivation for my work. Most of my pieces are carved in wax. I start by studying a hand, an insect, a bird. I also look at field guides and books on animal anatomy. I make sketches and models; it's a very intense learning process. Then I start to carve in wax—I use dental tools, wax pen, alcohol lamp, and, of course, different kinds of wax. Sometimes I even paint with wax to create a special surface. I worked on the forelegs of the praying mantis over a two-week period. The entire insect took six months to complete. I carved the Head earrings over a period of six months. The hands each take me about two weeks—I am now working on a baby's hands, with dimples.

technique

EARRINGS *Beetle*
Sterling silver
Cast

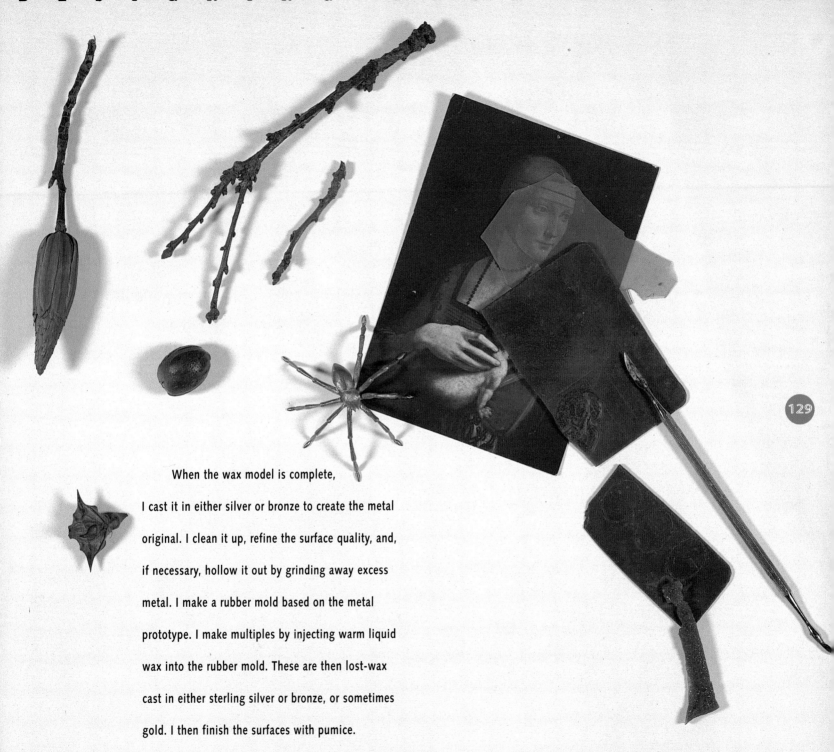

When the wax model is complete,
I cast it in either silver or bronze to create the metal
original. I clean it up, refine the surface quality, and,
if necessary, hollow it out by grinding away excess
metal. I make a rubber mold based on the metal
prototype. I make multiples by injecting warm liquid
wax into the rubber mold. These are then lost-wax
cast in either sterling silver or bronze, or sometimes
gold. I then finish the surfaces with pumice.

KISS

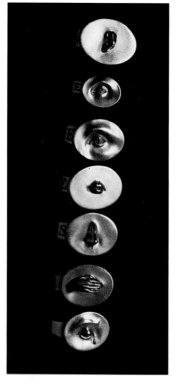

RINGS *Love Token*
10-karat gold
Cast

PIN *Praying Mantis*
Oxidized bronze
Cast

gabriella kiss

COMB *Fly*
18-karat gold and horn
Cast and carved

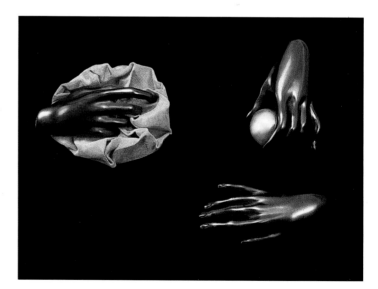

PINS *Hand*
Oxidized and gold-plated bronze
Cast

EARRINGS   *Bird Head with Egg*
18-karat gold and turquoise
Cast

EARRINGS   *Articulated Wasp*
18-karat gold and horn
Cast and carved

EARRINGS   *Head*
Sterling silver
Cast

RINGS

Inscription and Medieval Stone
Gold and colored stones
Cast

CUFF   *Blade of Grass with Leafhoppers*
22-karat gold, oxidized bronze, and black pearls
Cast

Catherine Butler sees the human body as a stage animated by lively, energetic people, birds, bugs, and spirits. The expressive figures in her jewelry express the various moods and activities of everyday life.

In her one-of-a-kind and production jewelry, Butler makes a political comment as well as an aesthetic statement. Her life is defined by commitment: her jewelry is one element in a continuum, which has also included activism, radio programming, teaching, and collaborative installation and performance art. "As I confronted the issue of being a studio artist while the world seems to be in continual crises, my involvement in issues outside the studio found its way into my work as social commentary." Now with a family, home, and garden, her focus has changed, but not her sense of conviction. Her most recent work reflects humor and a delight in nature and fantasy.

Catherine Butler

As a student at the Cleveland Art Institute, Butler studied painting and film animation, but the jewelry studio claimed her. The excellent technical training and emphasis on good craftsmanship and design prepared her to be a studio artist. It was the ceramics department, however, that introduced Butler to the concept of production work—that an artist could earn a living making affordable work. She applied those lessons to her jewelry making.

Her work has evolved over the past fifteen years, from animated abstract forms to her signature figurative jewelry. The early figures were less anatomical, and the technique had a raw simplicity. Over the years the figures have become more articulated, refined, detailed, and dimensional. Clothing and accessories have grown more elaborate as Butler has acquired more stamping tools.

Butler has always used color and pattern to wonderful effect. Yet in her most recent work, she has consciously simplified her palette, using only silver to fabricate her whimsical sprites and insects. Eliminating color and pattern, she concentrates on the "cool warmth" of oxidized silver and on achieving more dimensional form. The restrained quality of the silver suits the otherworldliness of these imagined apparitions.

133

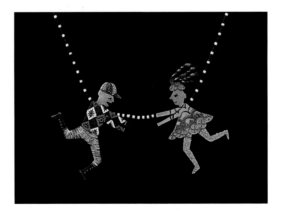

NECKLACE   *The Closer They Get . . .*
Sterling silver, copper, and brass
Pierced, formed, stamped, oxidized, and
inlaid with colored epoxy

PINS   *Balancing Act*
Copper and brass
Pierced, textured, and inlaid with colored epoxy

I think of my jewelry as drawings to be worn. I am continually fascinated by the possibilities of sheet metal and wire fabrication. In my earliest studio work, I was concerned with animating abstract forms—which soon gave way to figurative work. Certain motifs run through all my work: humor, patterns, the human figure, flower and plant forms, fish. Sprites, birds, imps, ants, garlic, fruit, and caryatids are recent additions to the

technique

production line. My interest in historical jewelry, decorative arts, gardening, and the circus also contribute to my designs.

My production work has always evolved out of my one-of-a-kind pieces. I don't sketch much. I often start by playing with scraps or a few premade parts. Then, all of a sudden, the concept takes shape.

134

PINS *People*
Copper, brass, and nickel silver
Pierced, stamped, and inlaid with colored epoxy

Some ideas bounce around in my head for years before they materialize in

a particular project. With the Fish series, I was able to indulge my love of

decorative patterns. By giving the fish human attributes, I could make

witty comments   about people. The leftover scraps of

patterned metal   from these pieces soon

rearranged themselves   into figures of people,

with their own stories to tell. These early pieces eventually

developed   into my production series jewelry. I work with nonferrrous

metals: silver, brass, copper, and nickel silver. I love taking flat sheet and

giving it dimension. I enjoy using simple, basic

techniques: sawing, drilling, piercing, stamping,

soldering, sanding, and bending with pliers. I choose

techniques appropriate to the material

and the statement I am trying to make.

135

BUTLER

EARRINGS
Fish
Sterling silver
and bronze
Pierced, stamped,
and inlaid with
colored epoxy

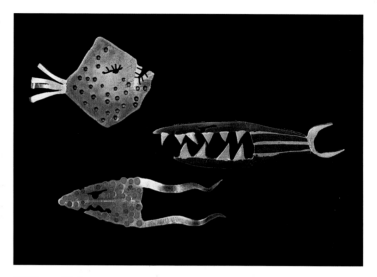

PINS *Fish*
Sterling silver and copper
Pierced, married metal, stamped, oxidized,
and inlaid with colored epoxy

catherine butler

NECKLACE *Exercise*
Copper, brass, and nickel silver
Pierced, stamped, oxidized, and inlaid with colored epoxy

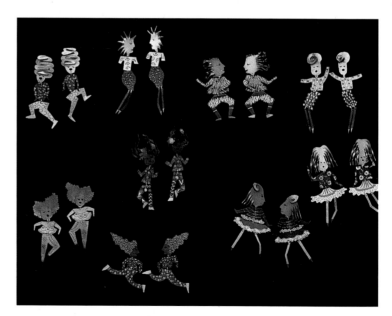

EARRINGS
Sleepwalker
Copper and brass
Pierced, oxidized

EARRINGS *Multi-articulated People*
Copper, brass, and nickel silver
Pierced, stamped, oxidized, and inlaid with colored epoxy

136

PINS *Ant*
Sterling silver
Pierced and oxidized

NECKLACE *Feeding the Birds*
Sterling silver, copper, brass, and glass beads
Pierced, formed, stamped, oxidized, and inlaid with
colored epoxy

PIN SETS *Volleyball*
Brass and nickel silver
Pierced, formed, stamped, oxidized,
and inlaid with colored epoxy

137

EARRINGS *Caryatids*
Sterling silver, copper, and brass
Pierced, formed, and oxidized

PINS
Hairdo
Sterling silver
and brass
Pierced, formed,
and oxidized

Contributors

Abrasha
P.O. Box 640283
San Francisco, CA 94109

Michael Good Design
P.O. Box 788
Rockport, ME 04856

Amy Anthony
1211 Titus Avenue
Rochester, NY 14617

Lorelei Hamm
153 Garfield Place #4L
Brooklyn, NY 11215

Catherine A. Butler
3014 East Overlook
Cleveland Heights, OH 44118-2438

Barbara Heinrich
P.O. Box 503
Pittsford, NY 14534

Jocelyn Chateauvert
123 1st Avenue South
Mount Vernon, IA 52314

Reiko Ishiyama
252 West 30th Street #9B
New York, NY 10001

Peggy Eng
P.O. Box 63146
Saint Louis, MO 63163

John Iversen
53 Crosby Street
New York, NY 10012

Mary Kanda
39 Leonard Street
Gloucester, MA 01930

Boo Poulin
36 Saint Paul #5W
Rochester, NY 14604

Gabriella Kiss
Millis Lane Box 596
Bangall, NY 12506

Didi Suydam
58 Willow Street
Providence, RI 02909

Thomas Mann
1810 Magazine Street
New Orleans, LA 70130

Kathryn L. Timmerman
P.O. Box 3072
La Jolla, CA 92038

Valerie Mitchell
120 South Vignes Street #403
Los Angeles, CA 90012

David Urso
862 Buck Road
Stone Ridge, NY 12484

Joan A. Parcher
165 Arlington Avenue
Providence, RI 02906

Ginny Whitney
175 West 76th Street #9A
New York, NY 10023

Galleries: United States

Albright Knox Art Gallery
1285 Elmwood Avenue
Buffalo, NY 14222
716 882 8700

American Artisan
4231 Harding Road
Nashville, TN 37205
615 298 4691

American Pie
327 South Street
Philadelphia, PA 19147
215 351 8100

Atypic
333 W. Brown Deer Road
Milwaukee, WI 53217
414 351 0333

Connell Gallery
333 Buckhead Avenue
Atlanta, GA 30305
414 261 1712

De Novo
250 University Avenue
Palo Alto, CA 94301
415 327 1256

Fireworks
210 First Avenue South
Seattle, WA 98104
206 682 8707

Freehand
8413 West Third Street
Los Angeles, CA 90048
213 655 2607

Gallery I/O
1812 Magazine Street
New Orleans, LA 70130
504 581 2111

Jewelers' Werk Galerie
2000 Pennsylvania Ave., NW
Washington, DC 20006
202 293 0249

Joanne Rapp Gallery
The Hand and the Spirit
4222 North Marshall Way
Scottsdale, AR 85251
602 949 1262

Linda Richman Jewelry at
Katie Gingrass Gallery
241 N. Broadway
Milwaukee, WI 53202
414 289 0855

Mindscape
1506 Sherman Avenue
Evanston, IL 60201
847 864 2660

Mobilia
358 Huron Avenue
Cambridge, MA 02138
617 876 2109

Motto
17 Brattle Street
Cambridge, MA 02138
617 868 8448

Museum of Modern Art
MOMA Store
44 West 53rd Street
New York, NY 10019
212 708 9700

Nancy Margolis Gallery
367 Fore Street
Portland, ME 04101
207 775 3822

Nancy Sachs Gallery
7700 Forsyth
St. Louis, MO 63105
314 727 7770

Nina Liu & Friends
24 State Street
Charleston, SC 29401
803 722 2744

Objects of Desire Gallery
3704 Lexington Road
Louisville, KY 40207
502 896 2398

Philip David
968 Farmington Avenue
West Hartford, CT 06107
203 232 6979

Pistachio's
One East Delaware
Chicago, IL 60611
312 988 9433

Ragazzi's Flying Shuttle
607 First Avenue
Seattle, WA 98104
206 343 3101

San Francisco Museum
   of Modern Art
151 Third Street
San Francisco, CA 94103
415 357 4000

Shaw Gallery
100 Main Street
Northeast Harbor, ME 04662
207 276 5000

Susan Cummins Gallery
12 Miller Avenue
Mill Valley, CA 94941
415 383 1512

Takashimaya
693 Fifth Avenue
New York, NY 10022
800 753 2038

Twist
30 NW 23rd Place #101
Portland, OR 97210
503 224 0334

The Works
303 Cherry Street
Philadelphia, PA 19106
215 922 7775

Galleries: International

Artwalk
Piazza Motta 1
6612 Ascona
Switzerland

Barneys Japan Co. Ltd.
3-14-1 Shijuku-ku
Tokyo 160
Japan

Designers Guild
277 Kings Road
London SW35En
England

Electrum Gallery
21 South Moulton Street W1
London
England

Galerie V+V
Bauernmarkt 19
1010 Vienna
Austria

Rox/Pithelwaite & Row-Thorpe
61 1A Barnscleuth Square
Elizabeth Bay (Sydney), NSW
Australia

Sandra Ainsley Gallery
Exchange Tower 2
1st Canadian Place, Box 262
Toronto, Ontario
Canada M5X1B5

Shelley Tadman Gallery
408 Academy Road
Winnipeg, Manitoba
Canada R3N0B9

Spektrum
Turkenstr. 37, Ruckgebaude
80799 Munich
Germany